High Impact Educators

High Impact Educators

How Graduates Describe Their Best Teachers

John Elling Tufte and
Brenda Tufte

ROWMAN & LITTLEFIELD
Lanham • Boulder • New York • London

Published by Rowman & Littlefield
An imprint of The Rowman & Littlefield Publishing Group, Inc.
4501 Forbes Boulevard, Suite 200, Lanham, Maryland 20706
www.rowman.com

6 Tinworth Street, London SE11 5AL, United Kingdom

British Library Cataloguing in Publication Information Available

Library of Congress Cataloging-in-Publication Data

Names: Tufte, John E. (John Elling), 1972- author. | Tufte, Brenda, 1965- author.
Title: High impact educators : how graduates describe their best teachers / John Elling Tufte, Brenda
    Tufte.
Description: Lanham : Rowman & Littlefield Publishers, 2021. | Includes bibliographical references.
    | Summary: "What educational experiences have helped college graduates to successfully com-
    plete their degrees and prepare for their chosen careers? What motivates them to be curious and
    confident learners throughout their lives? This book examines these questions and more through
    seminal research and in-depth interviews of 150 college freshmen, college seniors, and recently
    hired college graduates across the United States. These first-hand accounts-including what
    helped them overcome their gaps and achieve success, brought fresh surprises. How should we
    teach to prepare graduates with the needed knowledge, skills, and dispositions to thrive? What
    learning opportunities are needed for students to have the capacity to think critically and solve
    problems in the 21st Century? The authors are excited to reveal what high school and college
    graduates shared about how their teachers and professors impacted their learning and achieve-
    ment. This book gives teachers, professors, parents, and administrators seeking to understand
    effective instructional strategies and models for today's students, a framework that analyzes
    current research and forms a deeper inquiry starting in the front row seats of America's class-
    rooms. How do high school and college graduates describe high-impact educators and learning?
    We finally asked"-- Provided by publisher.
Identifiers: LCCN 2021003942 (print) | LCCN 2021003943 (ebook) | ISBN 9781475839890 (cloth) |
    ISBN 9781475839906 (paperback) | ISBN 9781475839913 (epub)
Subjects: LCSH: College teachers--Rating of--United States. | College students--Attitudes--United
    States. | Teacher-student relationships--United States. | Motivation in education--United States.
Classification: LCC LB2333 .T84 2021 (print) | LCC LB2333 (ebook) | DDC 378.1/25--dc23
LC record available at https://lccn.loc.gov/2021003942
LC ebook record available at https://lccn.loc.gov/2021003943

This book is dedicated to our children, Dexter, Dylan, Natalie, and Duncan, whose lives continue to be shaped by high-impact educators and the importance of a lifelong education.

Contents

Acknowledgments

The research for this book would not have been possible without the generous assistance of leaders in colleges and universities across the nation who supported us as we conducted student interviews on their campuses. Their kind hospitality and aid in connecting with their institutional review boards, reserving interview space and times on campus, and warmly welcoming us into their communities was instrumental to creating a platform for students to share their experiences and perspectives.

We extend sincere gratitude to the college freshmen, seniors, and newly hired graduates who shared their valuable time reflecting on their educational experiences. Their honest feedback about influences that led to their successes in college and the workplace highlighted the critical impact of skilled, caring teachers and professors.

Introduction

How Graduates Define High-Impact Educators and Learning

High school and college graduates are entering an era where change will confront them at an unprecedented pace. To thrive in this era, graduates must be critical thinkers who are nimble in their ability to adapt and apply their current knowledge and skills to emerging challenges. The educators preparing students to navigate continuous change must evolve with the same iterative mindset they hope to develop in their students. Times have changed—on that, we agree.

Educators and stakeholders in K–12 and higher education considering the question of how the world has changed in the past two to three decades have no problem identifying rampant changes. Digitization, social issues, globalization, demographic shifts, and urbanization are some of the factors that have led to broadly recognized and important changes in society. The question is not *do* we need to change our educational approaches for the demands of the twenty-first century, but *how*.

How should we teach in order to prepare graduates with the needed knowledge, skills, and dispositions to thrive? What pedagogical shifts are necessary, and what long-held educational practices continue to be effective? As educators, policymakers, and stakeholders weigh in with research, evidence-based recommendations, and strong personal beliefs, a multitude of models have emerged.

In some districts and universities, educational practices are so deeply entrenched within the institutional cultures that change over the past half-century is virtually undetectable. Within these varied groups of traditionalists, some have floundered in their failure to agree on a vision or rally needed change. Others have purposefully stayed the course, skeptical of some contemporary strategies and confident in traditional models such as classical education or teacher-centered delivery of instruction.

Among innovators, the pace and scope of change vary widely. Some institutions have evolved gradually, beginning with a distinct shift from knowledge-based approaches to skills-based approaches. Many combine direct instruction with active learning. These include differentiated instruction, project-based learning, and collaborative inquiry in a more learner-centered environment. Others have turned the industrial model on its head and fundamentally dismantled subject silos, learning spaces, and even age-matched grade levels, temporal credit units, and grade point averages for an individualized, standards-based approach that fully personalizes learning.

Whichever end of the spectrum within this continuum of educational reform, pedagogical practices are being closely scrutinized to understand which strategies move the assessment needle and best prepare graduates for success in the twenty-first century. The number of variables involved is vast—from curriculum, schedule, educators, parents, and student readiness to funding, facilities, and resources.

Grabbing at fads and frosting from the latest landscape of education innovation can be as risky as failing to evolve with the society for which we are preparing our graduates. In the field of education, the stakes cannot be overstated. Because of the unique needs of learners, institutions, cultures, and content areas, what works in one geographical area won't necessarily work in another.

Effective education calls for educational leaders to provide a filter that considers their student needs, faculty, resources, and vision. Sharing innovative approaches and student data can reveal patterns that lead to success for critical consideration of how they might be adapted to meet student needs. Technology has allowed the sharing of effective educational practices to extend beyond local schools and universities to a global platform.

In addition, recent advancements in educational neuroscience research have taught us about how the brain learns as well as the uniqueness of each learner. In response to neuroscience research, educators are called to utilize effective pacing and multisensory teaching, employ scaffolded repetition, and tap into student interests and readiness. We know, or at least we think we know, that in order to motivate students and facilitate encoding, strategies such as establishing relevance, harnessing emotion in positive ways, attending to mindfulness, engaging students, and fostering creativity are helpful.

Both behaviorist and neuroscience research have provided evidence to suggest that personalizing curriculum and instruction is beneficial. If educators can target zones of proximal development and build rich schemata and background knowledge while designing opportunities to connect concepts to existing schemas, lasting learning is more likely. The relational nature of learning reminds us that supportive mentoring and positive classroom environments abundant in opportunities for collaboration are potent influences.

Meta-analyses of empirical research, including John Hattie's landmark meta-analyses, provide multiple data points about which interventions appear to work and under what conditions they work best. Hattie documented that strategies such as formative feedback, student self-assessment, response to intervention, reciprocal teaching, teacher clarity, problem-based learning, metacognition embedded into content instruction, and direct instruction followed by guided and independent practice all appear to have a positive bearing on student achievement. Also, teacher efficacy and extended professional learning for teachers in the form of micro-teaching, collaboration with colleagues and outside experts, and teacher engagement during the professional learning process seem to strengthen teaching and student learning.[1]

As we glean truths from behaviorism, neuroscience research, educators, student assessment data, and the sharing of educational models and instructional strategies, we know what educators and researchers think good teaching looks like. However, we don't often study what students think great teaching looks like. That important perspective rises only by closely examining the unique experiences from the vantagepoint of students within our educational system.

Recent graduates, unlike their elementary counterparts, are capable of critical reflection about their learning. As we shape educational models for a new era, our architecture should be informed by the voices, learning experiences, and performance of the graduates who have been the participants of pedagogical initiatives.

The reason educational trends ebb and flow is often because of our misconceptions about the delivery and effectiveness of these trends. We sometimes have the perception that we see improvement when we merely see change. Amid innovation, leaders, including those closest to the work and the students, must be observant, reflective, and critical of the initiative's impact, including long-term and unintended consequences.

Continuous improvement, together with a willingness to rethink, rewind, or revamp, is the responsibility of all of us. What knowledge, concepts, and skills are needed for students to have the capacity to think critically and solve problems in the twenty-first century? What motivates graduates to be curious and confident learners throughout their lives? What impacts have educational experiences had for students? When we are dealing with college and high school graduates, nothing *we* think matters if it didn't matter for them.

Research for this book was conducted over two years with interviews of high school and college graduates spanning from December 2018 to September 2019. Graduates from eleven states participated in interviews that were conducted in two phases. In phase 1, researchers interviewed college freshmen and college seniors.

First-year college students shared perspectives on their K–12 teachers and learning experiences that got them to their freshman college year and reflected on the strengths and gaps that were apparent during their first year of college. College seniors shared perspectives on their K–12 and college professors as well as the learning experiences that contributed to their triumphant arrival to their senior year of college and reflected on where they felt prepared or ill-prepared for entering their careers.

In phase 2 of the study, researchers interviewed the group of graduates best positioned to give perspectives on educators and educational experiences that impacted their career readiness—recently hired college graduates. Reflecting with a broader lens than their counterparts still in college, graduates who had been working between one and three years following graduation shared perspectives on professors and learning experiences that contributed to their success in the workplace.

In the final phase of the study, interviews were transcribed and coded, and the emerging themes were then identified and analyzed. Perhaps the most surprising finding was the consistency in which the main issues emerged among all three interview groups. The most prevalent themes that arose from the data inform the chapters of this book.

The book is divided into three parts. Part 1, "Impacting Student Success," explores the critical vs. peripheral aspects that influence teaching and learning and unpacks what high-impact educators do that sets them apart and resonates with their students, years, even decades later. Part 2, "The Ever-Growing List of Twenty-First-Century Skills," discusses the formation and evidence of critical thinking, creativity initiated by curiosity, collaboration, autonomy, communication, determination, growth mindset, and character.

Part 3, "Relationships and Student Growth," examines relationships and the formation of student academic and personal growth. When relationships emphasized academic and personal growth and conveyed belief in the student's ability to flourish in the future, the impact of relationships, we consistently observed, was lasting and profound.

Each chapter begins with what graduates said, followed by a discussion of what it means for educators, and ends with closing perspectives. The first-hand accounts of students and ways with which they align or challenge what we think we know about their learning experiences brought fresh surprises. We are excited to reveal what high school and college graduates shared about how their teachers and professors impacted their learning.

This book gives teachers, professors, parents, and administrators seeking to understand effective instructional strategies and models for today's students a framework that analyzes current research and forms a deeper inquiry starting in the front-row seats of U.S. classrooms from the defining voices of students. How do high school and college graduates define high-impact educators and learning? We finally asked.

NOTE

1. Hattie, J. (2015). "The applicability of Visible Learning to higher education." *Scholarship of Teaching and Learning in Psychology,* 1(1), 79–91.

I

Impacting Student Success

ONE

Critical Versus Peripheral

FOOLING OURSELVES

What makes the process of educating students productive and ultimately successful? What moves the needle in K–12 schools and universities? What, exactly, causes the ever-essential yet remarkably elusive "student growth" elite educators demand from their work?

These questions and many others drove the research leading to this book. Student growth provides a multitude of challenges for educators at all levels, for at its feet sits one initiative after another, each capable of mystifying even the savviest of teachers. Educational initiatives can be tricky because they often come packaged as critical twenty-first-century requirements for school quality. To make the picture even cloudier, there is often nothing whatsoever wrong with the latest innovations set before educators—except that if viewed as a panacea, they can distract educators from that which causes actual student growth.

Leaders in education often mistakenly tackle what is hoped, perhaps even what is believed to lead to student growth. With this panacean approach, there is an excellent chance that the focus of educating students is centered on a peripheral, assuming that emphasizing it (and likely a few other peripheral factors) will lead to favorable results.

How can high-impact educators know if something is peripheral? K–12 and university leaders often struggle to identify and subsequently separate the critical from the peripheral in schools, and that is the point.

Many in education have personal beliefs about teaching style, for example. K–12 leaders, perhaps, feel strongly about filling hallways and classrooms with outgoing, high-energy, extrovert teachers who instruct with a booming voice, a quick wit, incredible relationship-building skills, and a personal touch.

These teachers could deliver a powerful lecture on the secession of the Civil War or run-on sentences or the periodic table. They are truly great and are adept at engaging students and facilitating collaborative groups that demonstrate the incredible potential of peer teaching and learning.

Technology has revolutionized our lives and, albeit delayed in most schools, has also transformed education. We know the world is evolving, and we want—we demand—that our students graduate with as many technological advantages as possible. This highly networked, modern world demands of its successful participants the technological skillset to compete on a global level. What good are we, after all, if we are not a one-to-one school?

Equally transformational has been the distinct shift in school culture. We believe to our core that it is good for our students to be in a personalized environment. Everyone learns best when we are relaxed and stress-free, we believe, and we translate these ideologies to break the mold of the conventional agrarian school model and expectations. Homework, assignment due dates, tardies, and school etiquette expectations need to be reimagined and reinvented, for what can we expect to accomplish with twenty-first-century students if we treat them like kids of the 1980s?

Certainly, the architecture and physical design of schools must evolve to reflect innovative models of teaching and learning. Educational leaders have heard from business and community leaders that collaboration and creativity are king in today's professional world. Hearing this, we find ourselves reimagining the physical and temporal structures in our K–12 and collegiate environments (often contracted to one or more of the business leaders emphasizing community partnerships) to support student and teacher flexibility, creativity, and collaboration. Movable walls, student-friendly furniture, and adaptable spaces are desired to meet the multifaceted needs of contemporary learners and innovative pedagogical models.

If we are lucky, we have funding enough to build or renovate learning spaces to look much different than their twentieth-century counterparts. We equip our student body with electronic devices as we reimagine our approach to running a classroom. In a time when student anxiety is at an all-time high, we do the best we can to reduce stress and unreasonable discomfort from the school environment. Knowing the unparalleled rate of change our students will face in this new global world, we strive to integrate content and equip them with the transferable skills needed to flourish outside the classroom.

Does it work? It depends.

Educators can attempt all of the above and more, and if the administrators, professors, and teachers are great, these peripherals likely do play a role in student growth. Consequently, there is no need for schools to seek low-energy, worksheet-giving teachers with a predilection for showing movies five days a week.

We need not reclaim the students' laptops and venture back to the Dewey Decimal System for our primary research methodology. Teachers should not feel obligated to abolish collaboration practices and instead keep students in rows and lecture halls for eight hours a day or revert back to requiring the fifteen-pound wooden artifact potty pass to and from the restroom.

Most of the peripherals in the K–12 and university settings are not harmful. We are obligated, however, to know the difference between those *peripheral* educational issues and trends and what is *critical* for student growth. If we confuse one for the other, *student growth* will be more the product of good fortune, not the result of a quality education provided by high-impact educators.

FROM THE MOUTHS OF GRADUATES

When asked to speak about both what best prepared them for success in college or the workforce and in what ways they were not adequately developed for these arenas, those interviewed for this book (over 150 students in eleven states) offered profound as well as ironic insights with what they did *not* address:

- teaching style
- classroom activities
- fun
- technology
- facilities

This is not to suggest that teaching style is irrelevant, that any approach in the classroom will suffice for student growth. We are not to interpret from these student interviews, furthermore, that recent graduates preferred misery over fun while learning—or that it was quite fine to have leaky roofs and moldy carpet causing illness throughout their academic careers.

It does communicate, however, that issues like teaching style, activities, and the use of technology have become assumptions for today's college-bound students. These are *peripherals*, almost universally unworthy of reference for recent graduates as factors for substantial student growth.

One interviewed student epitomized this reality to the point of leaving the authors of this book speechless. This student, a young man one semester into his college career, shared that he attended a parochial high school before college—and that he studied a Classical Core Curriculum consisting of reading (classics), writing, arithmetic, and Latin. Furthermore, his school did not allow computers.

Hearing from an 18-year-old in 2019 that he had not used a computer for academics until he reached college more than justifies a few follow-up questions. *How is this even possible? How out-of-touch are the graduates of this school? Is this young man even capable of contributing to the research for this book?* All of these questions and more ran through the researchers' minds as they heard the interviewee explain his high school experiences. Eventually, questions were offered: "Was it a difficult adjustment for you? I assume you have needed to submit assignments online, right? Have you been able to keep up?"

His response was unforgettable: "Yeah, it was super-hard . . . and it's weird to use my laptop for everything now."

One of the researchers leaned forward, nearly incapable of disguising her excitement for what most certainly would follow, a fantastic example of how essential it is to equip students with twenty-first-century technology skills (a fully acknowledged bias). She waited.

The young man elaborated. He explained that it took a while to grow accustomed to submitting work via his campus's learning management system (LMS), that he still needs reminding that not all of his instructors use technology or expect technology use from him the same way. His most significant challenge, however, was learning how to navigate the university's site for the multitude of chores it contains, such as parking registration, financial aid reports, billing, registration, and the like. With this, he explained that there is an additional challenge of remembering to check his email for notices from the university.

"Gosh, how long did it take you to figure any of that out? Did you seek help from someone in the university, someone from the tech department?" The young man's eyes got big as he exhaled with an acknowledging expression. He was nodding in agreement. "Yeah, I mean, I had to have my roommate sit down with me for like 20 minutes that first week so I could figure out how to do all of that stuff."

Twenty minutes. This young man enrolled in a university, was performing well at the trail end of his first semester, and had virtually no previous experience using a computer for schoolwork before his roommate sat down to give a twenty-minute tutorial on the ins and outs of his university's LMS.

How is this possible? It is possible because, although the use of a laptop for academics, a parking pass, and assignment submission was foreign to him, basic twenty-first-century technology skills were not. He knew enough to turn it on, follow directions, ask questions, and figure it out from there. Technology is a *peripheral*.

He was asked in the interview about what contributed to his learning, his growth, his improvement, his college readiness, and so forth. Technology was not worth his reference until the researchers learned of his unique high school experience. Even then, his explanation of the unique set of circumstances amounted to nothing more than a footnote. Like nearly every other participant for this study, he used the interview to describe positive, purposeful human interaction, whether with parents or educators, as the catalyst for his growth.

It can be tempting for educators to become passionate about the "stuff" in education, the one-to-one technology, the new project-based lesson plans, the user-friendly spaces. These can be wonderful, to be certain, but these are *peripherals*. The high-impact educators themselves are *critical*.

EDUCATIONAL INNOVATION

Twenty-first-century facilities, cutting-edge technology, and a fun, welcoming environment can play an immeasurable role in the education of our K–12 and college students. However, all of these qualities can also be found at the YMCA. Peripherals can be present in classrooms, lecture halls, or labs, replete with fun and excitement and super-fast Wi-Fi—with not much learning. The critical focus of this book, as detailed by those interviewed, centers around high-impact educators. Their methods, it seems, are as varied as their students' needs.

Both K–12 and higher education have become perfect targets for those championing innovation. In the last two decades, the testing business alone has tripled, now exceeding $3 billion a year. The assessment money trail, spurred mostly by accreditation and accountability requirements, has been closely followed by a host of private companies offering high-priced, aligned curriculum and technology, all packaged in the form of a noun. In a nation with over 6 million kindergarten- through college-level educators, a handful of companies control the lion's share of a market that dominates every budget line item for instruction and is developed without input from the most highly skilled educators.

At all levels, we spend an astonishing amount of money on the peripheral. Furthermore, the long-term results of our investments essentially go unchecked after students graduate from our institutions. Educators must be cautious about how innovation is defined and measured. The assumption, particularly from those selling it, is that the change is necessary, the change is past-due, and the change is for the better.

It can be. With the right professors, teachers, and administrators overseeing educational innovations, student growth can be the most significant result. Nevertheless, if innovation remains nothing more than a program, a sales-pitch response to required standards, funding cuts, or garnering recognition, for example, education suffers. Educational innovation is useful if, and only if, it results in student growth.

This is a challenge in education. What constitutes student growth? Test scores? Placement on a proficiency scale? We have listened to that fight for decades, and no one has changed his or her mind about what the scores reveal. Culture, climate, and attendance? Our experience tells us that if students come to school more, they will learn more. However, this cannot be our only weapon—if being happier and being present were the fool-proof keys to student growth, Netflix and Instagram would be the best teachers on Earth. We know better.

The researchers for this book interviewed the most successful students, those who were either beginning their college careers, nearly graduating from college, or new to the workforce after college graduation. Whatever student growth is and however it can or should be measured, the interviewed participants for this book have demonstrated it. As for effective educational innovation, these participants outlined what significant changes are needed (and what should not change) by defining high-impact educators and how these people have made student growth a reality.

TWO

High-Impact Educators

AVERAGE IS FORGOTTEN

The research for this book consisted of over 150 interviews with college students and recent college graduates new to the workforce. These freshmen, seniors, and newly employed were asked an array of questions and prompts, as unguided as possible, with a goal of finding pronounced themes about what played significant roles in their development and successes. A sampling of the interview questions follows:

- Why did you choose to become a college student?
- What helped get you to this point in your academic or professional career?
- To what extent do you feel you are/were prepared for college homework?
- In what areas did you feel most underprepared for success in college?
- What approaches or strategies to learning have helped you be successful?
- When and how did you learn these strategies?
- Describe the most effective teacher or professor you have met. What did this educator accomplish? How did he or she do it?

Those interviewed for this research answered these questions and many others by describing three groups of adults above any other people, strategies, philosophies, initiatives, or educational peripherals: loving parents, ineffective teachers and professors, and high-impact teachers and professors. Not one participant for this study referenced an average parent or teacher. Average, it seems, is forgotten.

Ineffective educators, as conveyed by college students and recent graduates, are remembered for failing to so much as accomplish what they are contracted to do: teach content. These educators were described as sometimes affable (sometimes not), often intelligent, and even quite busy in the school setting. Participants noted that some of their ineffective educators coached a sport or two, supervised the prom committee, and helped with the student council. These educators were often truly good people, according to those interviewed. However, they were described as educators who did not teach the content or associated skills or prepare the interviewed students for success after high school or college graduation. Several students described their worst teachers as not being invested in their learning. Whether describing the teacher's unavailability to meet with them outside of class, the teacher's lack of belief in the student's ability to succeed in course, or the college professor not knowing their name, these dissentaneous relationships were consistently identified as an obstacle that impacted their motivation and shook their confidence within and even beyond the course.

High-impact educators, on the other hand, were described over and over, across the ranges of eleven states and among college freshman, college seniors, and recent college graduates as those who possess three qualities above anything and everything else:

1. They are content experts.
2. They are teaching experts.
3. They are relationship experts.

Interestingly, interviewed participants provided little to no description of high-impact educators beyond these three traits. Some spoke highly of their current professors, detailing in amazement how they could simultaneously show their brilliance while managing an auditorium full of college students—and somehow still manage to remember a student's name when confronted with an unscheduled office visit.

Others spoke about "that teacher" in high school, the one who at first seemed like a grouch, the one whose persistence wore on students like impending doom. This teacher was not there to win the faculty award for best Halloween costume; he or she had nothing whatsoever to add to the conversation about the homecoming king and queen nominations. This teacher taught difficult content, and the students were, like it or not, going to learn it. Interviewees described "that teacher" as someone who they knew they could rely on, someone who pushed them beyond their current state and believed in their ability to succeed.

Others, although years removed from childhood, referenced middle school or elementary teachers. One participant, a college senior, sat with tears in her eyes as she described an elementary teacher who "knew her," who saw something in her that no one else saw, who inspired her to do great things with her life. How? This teacher refused to allow the interviewed participant to remain a poor reader. With a semester remaining in college, this young woman could no longer be described as being below-average at anything academically.

Content knowledge, teaching skills, and relationships. Part 3 of this book addresses the relationships–student growth correlation, but for the purpose of defining high-impact educators, a few notes are worth emphasis. The interviewed participants did not describe a particular person that college deans or K–12 administrators could recognize from 50 yards away and subsequently hire before sundown. Age, gender, sexual orientation, interests, hobbies, clothing style, sense of humor, left-wing, right-wing, attractiveness, and the like—these were irrelevant for the interviewees describing their most impactful educators. Interviewed participants for this book either did not know this information, or it was not worth describing.

Furthermore, participants offered no insights about the role their most impactful teachers played in the process of university, department, district, or building goals, nor did they describe earned accolades or titles; those interviewed would likely have little to no concept of those they have deemed "the best" beyond their effectiveness as educators in the student-teacher setting. From the perspectives of recent graduates, high-impact educators know their content remarkably well, and they know how to work with students so that the content is learned. With this, they never quit.

Profoundly ineffective educators were mentioned sporadically throughout the interview process for this book. Average educators were not remembered. high-impact educators, it seems, cannot be forgotten.

STUDENT GROWTH

As described by the recent graduates interviewed for this book, high-impact educators are content knowledge, pedagogy, and relationship experts. These three immense skillsets remain educationally irrelevant, however, if not used together to achieve significant student growth in both curriculum attainment and positive habit development.

Student growth, however, has a measurement problem. Educational leaders at the university level and within K–12 districts often make one of two mistakes related to student growth: either they assume or hope it is occurring and subsequently choose not to focus on it, or they focus intently on measuring it in the moment via test scores, surveys, data rationalizing, and the like.

The latter is remarkably common in universities and school districts. Focusing on the here and now, the latest initiative, the need for innovation, our hopes, our opinions, and our feelings can and often do lead educational leaders to neglect the one area demanding attention: student growth.

Authentic student growth is difficult to assess or measure because it requires patience, discipline, and humility from educators. Student growth often begins its climb with small, sometimes immeasurable steps that start first by getting through the brain's intake filters. The opening or closing of those filters may be related to developmental, environmental, relational, physical, or emotional factors. The fruits of their successful activation may not always coincide with or be detected by a scheduled assessment.

The unique narrative of each student we interviewed served as a poignant reminder that one size does not fit all when it comes to learning and growth and that to truly understand the needs of students, educators must know them. It may seem an impossible task when many educators teach well over a hundred students each year, but countless students we interviewed described their best educators as those who knew them and believed in them.

Educational neuroscientists would not be surprised at this description of the most impactful educators. Consider the brain's first sensory-intake filter: the reticular activating system (RAS), which receives millions of sensory inputs every second, but allows just a fraction to pass through as it protects against perceived threats with a fight, flight, or freeze response. The gatekeeping power of the survival-focused RAS filter, as well as the complex management function of the prefrontal cortex—including attention, decision-making, and emotional responses—illustrate the complex and relational nature of learning.[1] This complexity has many implications for the classroom, starting with the need to know our students.

Reducing students' fear of embarrassment or failure is vital to facilitate learning. This requires trusting relationships and supportive learning environments. Within those environments, neuroscience research has revealed teaching strategies effective in activating RAS, including visuals, novelty, engagement, multisensory input, and student choice, to name a few. Having used many of these with success, the researchers of this book sought to learn more about which were particularly helpful to student growth.

Interviewees recall with incredible clarity their triumphs in overcoming challenges and growing in their learning. Even small moments such as "finally understanding what to do with letters in an equation" or "not freezing when I read something that made *zero* sense to me" were vividly recalled. These triumphs were consistently traced back to high-impact educators who went the extra mile with a variety of strategies to help students make sense of new learning. Students remembered and referenced the significance of caring and passionate educators who reduced threat of failure, not by making it easy or fun, but by being there to support them in learning difficult concepts and skills—sometimes "one more time" and sometimes "in a different way."

The strategies educators used were varied, but they had in common a commitment to doing whatever it took to help students grow in their learning. Analysis of interview data also revealed that the resultant growth was not from teacher effort alone. The reciprocal nature of students' relationships with high-impact educators resulted in students' motivation to focus, work, and trust their teacher's feedback to meet the challenges and grow, even when they initially struggled. Frustration was reduced when students knew that they would have help in acquiring the understanding needed to move forward.

Self-efficacy grew with each success—whether that was in cycling back to master prerequisite knowledge or skills, reaching end-term learning targets, or merely moving significantly toward those targets. High-impact educators are focused on student growth and finding ways to promote input to the prefrontal cortex to help students latch on to each increment of growth and continue climbing.

Understanding that the value of an education often reveals itself long after the lessons aligned with curriculum or habit development have been delivered, the authors of this book opted to research educator quality by speaking with those who have graduated from high school, are attending college, or have graduated from college, and have thereupon amassed some perspective.

WHO ARE THE HIGH-IMPACT EDUCATORS?

Going into the research process for this book, the authors were confident they could adequately if not easily outline effective teaching strategies. Those of us with a significant career in education know the look of a great teacher when we see one, it was believed. Although effective teaching and remarkable educators struggle to fit onto a scale, those of us "in the know" believe we see great teaching the way we feel love—we just *know*.

For these researchers, some of this rings true. The interviewed participants for this book did not relocate education's North Star with their contributions; the authors are not struggling to comprehend what they heard from high school and college graduates. Rather, the participants for this book offered nuances that experienced educators may miss for being deeply entrenched in the day-to-day realities of doing what we believe is best for students and student growth. There is a difference, the researchers learned, between knowing we are loved and knowing what, exactly, we do that causes us to be loved.

Most educators understand the importance of knowing the content, the curriculum. Teaching grammar and sentence structure is rather futile when the teacher has little command of comma usage, independent clauses, dependent clauses, and the associated punctuation. Failing in this regard results in moving students forward in school without the content knowledge (age-appropriate grammar and sentence structure skills) necessary for success. This makes sense; it is obvious.

We also recognize that knowing the Pythagorean Theorem comes with no guarantee that students will learn it or its relevance to mathematical practices requiring its mastery. Educators must know the content, and they must know the pedagogical skills required to ensure that students learn and apply the content. This makes sense; it is obvious.

Lastly, whether it was inherently present in our teaching or we grew to realize its worth over time, we know that relationships matter in education. If we teach a sixth-grade boy who is struggling to find friends, his level of commitment to comprehending the relationship between comma usage and independent/dependent clauses will likely be lower than what is required to actually learn the material. We understand the filtration systems of the brain and that we need to know and care for the students if we want them to learn. This makes sense; it is obvious.

The participants for this study did not break any ground by outlining those three descriptions of a successful education. Most of us in education know this. What we did not know, however, was the extent to which these three areas (content knowledge, pedagogy, and relationships) matter to students, the incredible detail graduates described aligned to these areas, and how almost nothing else is of consequence for students when asked to describe those who best prepared them for future success.

The college freshman, college seniors, and recent college graduates interviewed for this book see the same forest educational leaders have been describing for years. At the same time, they also see trees that many educational leaders find indistinguishable from the hundreds or thousands of trees surrounding these. Our recent graduates recognize teacher qualities most of us have been too busy or too close to notice.

Within the interviews, it was apparent that college students and recent graduates understand the importance of content knowledge, pedagogical expertise, and relationships skills. What they provided was a highly focused, incredibly assented set of descriptors within those three qualities. The following are attributes and observations gleaned from the words of interviewed participants describing *high-impact educators*:

1. *High-impact educators (especially in the K–12 setting) are not always appreciated in the moment.* This message was delivered with clarity and regularity from the vast majority of those interviewed. The researchers were repeatedly offered story after story involving educators who insisted on student growth. Student growth, according to the participants, often requires temporary discomfort—and most K–12 students do not seek these moments. This, at times, requires discipline and trust in the teacher to avoid feeling over-

whelmed and incapacitated. The most impactful educators push students out of a comfort zone and then teach them how to accomplish while overcoming discomfort.

2. *High-impact educators know the difference between critical and peripheral educational issues.* In district or campus settings, with various philosophies, programs, and initiatives at hand, the most effective educators use a highly developed filter to separate what students need to grow (*critical*) from the multitude of various other educational obligations surrounding the profession (*peripheral*).

3. *High-impact educators have evolved to a level of excellence.* The teachers and professors described as most impactful have both a great deal of experience and, most likely, the habit of reflection. It takes time to become a high-impact educator; it takes trial and error and a dedication to learn what creates genuine student growth. The interviewed participants did not belittle neophyte teachers; they simply described seasoned, professional educators who were committed to excellence.

4. *High-impact educators act like adults.* This was made clear across the range of interviewed subjects regarding both K–12 teachers and college professors. Graduates did not describe their most impactful educators as cool, nor did they view them as friends. In fact, high-impact educators were described as more "parent-like" than as peers. They were labeled as smart, friendly, approachable, affable—and serious about their job. The participants for this book appreciated this combination, for it moved them to focus on growth.

5. *High-impact educators value class time, and they teach their students to do the same.* Again, this message from interviewed participants was consistent across the board. Their most impactful teachers do not waste the precious time they have with students. Fun? Maybe. Lighthearted? Perhaps. Regardless of classroom dynamics, students understand that class time is learning time when high-impact educators are leading.

6. *High-impact educators communicate well.* This runs the risk of being excessively obvious, for what is teaching if not communicating? Those interviewed, however, made proclamations about their most impactful teachers and their extraordinary ability to communicate with knowing both what to share with students and how to share it. They also communicated clearly about expectations. Yes, communication is what educators do for a living. With this approach, it could be offered that both the Beatles and the Monkeys were musical groups. All educators communicate; the most impactful are remembered for both the importance of the message and how effectively the message was delivered.

7. *High-impact educators are inquisitive.* No teachers are born with content knowledge. Pedagogical skills are not refined by accident. Harmonious and productive teacher-student relationships are not formed out of boredom. The most impactful educators make students curious not only because it helps them solve problems and will serve them well throughout their lives (although these are true) but also because the most impactful educators are themselves insatiably inquisitive. Why is it acceptable to occasionally write a fragmented sentence in academic writing? What happens when these two chemicals are combined and heated? What would have happened had JFK not been assassinated? What if everyone on earth jumped at the same time? High-impact educators explore, and their students notice.

8. *High-impact educators are persistent.* This theme was a hallmark within the interviews conducted. Droves of college students and recent graduates alike, when asked to think of the most effective educator they have known, referenced teachers or professors who would not stop working with them, not stop pushing them, not stop believing in them. These persistent high-impact educators make student growth their professional mantra, and this goal is not hindered by the reality that many or most students do not appreciate this while it is happening. Whether these educators know it or not, their persistence is often appreciated shortly thereafter and forevermore.

9. *High-impact educators make personal connections with each student, no matter how small a connection.* When speaking about their most impactful educators, participants spoke with specific details related to these educators knowing their content, knowing how to teach the content, and knowing them. This last part—the educators taking time to know the students—made a lasting impression on those interviewed for this book. Participants often laughed as they shared stories of "that teacher" who somehow remembered that Todd is this kid's older brother and that he joined the National Guard five years ago, that Abby's aunt was battling cancer a year ago, that Macey is a huge Twins fan, or that sometimes Dustin just needs a few minutes to decompress on Monday mornings. High-impact educators likely make connections of this ilk because it is in their being to do so whether the moments are remembered or forgotten. Nonetheless, these little things mean everything to some students—and that is where the seeds of student growth are sown.

WHAT IT MEANS

Chapter 1 compared peripherals to the critical in education. High-impact educators are not required to avoid the peripherals in schools or on campuses. In fact, many amazing teachers and professors invest themselves into what they know to be a peripheral—educational technology, for example. It makes sense that inquisitive and persistent educators aiming at maximizing student growth would invest time into educational technology, for if it is going to be used, it should be used with purpose.

All of that being true, based on the qualitative data collected via over 150 interviews from graduates covering eleven states combined with over fifty years of teaching experience from the authors of this book, there is an undeniable statement to be made about what, exactly, moves the needle in K–12 schools and universities: high-impact educators. As one participant superbly responded when asked about what has made her academic career so successful, "It's not what; it's who."

NOTE

1. D. A. Sousa, ed., *Mind, Brain, and Education: Neuroscience Implications for the Classroom* (Bloomington, IN: Solution Tree, 2010).

II

The Ever-Growing List of Twenty-First-Century Skills

THREE
Critical Thinking

SOLVING PROBLEMS

- Adaptable
- Decisive
- Confident
- Prepared
- Insightful
- Diplomatic
- Impartial
- Motivated
- Observant
- Resourceful
- Versatile
- Useful
- Helpful
- Self-aware
- Reasonable
- Intuitive
- Productive
- Accurate
- Effective
- Intelligent
- Empathetic

The terms above are descriptors given to adults who solve problems. They can *adapt* to varied conditions or situations, and they are *decisive* and *prepared*. They can *observe* a problem and *diplomatically* share their *insights* leading toward *reasonable* solutions. They are *helpful*, they are *intuitive*, and their *accuracy* has given them a track record of being *produc-*

tive. They solve problems, and the rest of us call them *intelligent* because of it.

But there is something more, something that lends itself to the existence of impressive critical thinking with all the requisite characteristics. Critically thinking problem-solvers are not born; they do not simply arrive on the scene with no backstory. They do not make things better without first learning a great deal and, then, being in countless positions to apply what they have learned. Problem-solvers, before anything else, are educated.

When our students are no longer our students, how will the education they have received be evident? We hope they are proficient readers, of course, that they prove capable of decoding and comprehending text of considerable sophistication. Whether they are responsible for NASA's spacecraft orbital data, analyzing data to determine the proper chemistry for this year's flu vaccine, or directly managing their personal finances, we hope our graduates possess an ability to conduct mathematical processes necessary for their adult life.

Of course, being skilled at reading and STEM, having a grasp of world history, or being well-spoken in multiple languages do not automatically make one a go-to for adult problem-solving. What can graduates do with what they know? The ability to apply their knowledge and skills matters immensely in the twenty-first century. To do this well, graduates must continuously build a bedrock of knowledge and skills and apply them often.

Communication matters. Reading matters. Math ability matters. And knowing that the Civil War happened in the United States . . . in the 1860s . . . and that President Lincoln was willing to be wildly unpopular to do what he knew was best . . . and that the country, despite nearly losing itself in an ash heap of both rage and sorrow, somehow found its way out to become better than it was before—it matters.

Why? Because problem-solvers are critical thinkers, and thinkers need an educational baseline, foundation of reading, writing, mathematics, history, communication, and other essential educational principles shared by educated adults. Problem-solvers *learn* to see multiple perspectives and solve problems. Without an adequate education, even the most motivated thinkers are limited in their ability to anticipate multiple perspectives, make connections, and generate solutions for complex predicaments.

The most impressive participants interviewed for this book, those who carry themselves as young people building a stellar collegiate record, a promising career, or both, have become scholars who take ownership of their learning. They ask:

1. What Can I "Do" with This Material?

Students who found the relevance of what they were learning and considered how it connected to further learning and to life were better prepared to apply it. Alex, a college senior shared,

> The teachers I have learned the most from were passionate about their content. . . . They cared about it and they talked about why it was important for all of us. They were always learning more and they wanted us to learn it too. They would give examples that made it relevant and interesting to discuss and think about. For me, it wasn't just about grades in those classes.

High-impact educators play a significant role in helping students interact with content and apply learning in meaningful ways. When learners were deliberate about establishing relevance, it allowed them to approach tasks such as the reading assigned for today's discussion, the historical significance of the Louisiana Purchase, the writing project due next week, the math equation posted on Google Classroom, or the psychological effects of losing a parent early in life, with greater purpose and broader ability to apply their learning to meaningful contexts.

Graduates referenced educators who took the time to share those contexts, asked or encouraged the right questions, and engaged students in learning that facilitated authentic application. A college biology major described her long-time "disinterest in all things science" until her sophomore year in high school when she had Mrs. Ennis for period 1 biology.

> I remember she had us dissecting a squid, and we located the ink sac which was super interesting because they release ink into the water to confuse their predators. Mrs. Ennis got all excited talking about phytoplankton, which form the food web for marine animals and are responsible for producing, like, half of the oxygen on the planet.

It was clear that this young lady was no longer disinterested in science.

> I mean, think about that. I did my semester project on the bioluminescent bacteria in the squid's light organs and the symbiotic relationship they share. . . . It piqued my interest in symbiotic relationships. Even when you're a teenager and no one gets you and you don't have any friends . . . here's your science teacher getting you excited about learning at 8:00 in the morning because she is so passionate about it and suddenly you are interested and curious and learning.

College seniors and recently-hired college graduates spoke often about the value of problem-solving activities as well as connections with professional mentors and internship experiences where they could apply their knowledge and skills.

When internships and interactions with professionals in their field were embedded into coursework early in their programs, the experiences often helped them find their strengths and areas of specialization. Like many of the college graduates we interviewed, a recently hired business and marketing major saw the pathway to his current job through a mentorship experience during his junior year.

> In Macro Technologies, they brought in a bunch of sales reps who invited us to their businesses. . . . They walked us through their daily work, their training programs, their recruiting programs, team building, and their daily projects. It was so valuable to merge the conceptual in the classroom to the tangible . . . the real meat and potatoes of the job.
>
> Prior to that, sales wasn't even on my radar but those experiences gave me a new direction. I added a sales certificate to my degree and started taking ownership for applying what I was learning to be successful in sales.

Critical thinkers consider why the learning matters—they want to own it. High-impact educators give them the experiences to get there.

2. How Can I Connect What I Am Learning to What I Already Know?

The students we visited had established at some point in their academic career (some earlier than others) a process that helps them make sense of new learning by attaching it to their own experiences and knowledge. One senior we spoke to was in the final semester of his engineering program and reflected back on a challenging freshman year when he was ready to quit.

> My freshman year was tough. I was enrolled in Calc and trig and Chem I and II all at the same time. One of my freshmen professors was awesome. . . . She clearly wanted us to succeed. . . . We did a lot of hands-on projects like solar ovens, portable inverters, and model bridges. . . . She'd have us test them for their strength compression and tension strength.

He noted that he and his classmates were

> doing things before we knew what we were doing, but for the first time I was applying what I had learned in my math and science classes and things started to click. When I connected things and analyzed, I could see, ahh . . . that's why that beam broke. That professor helped me stick through it and see the end goal of those early classes, even though at the time I felt like giving up.

Preparing graduates to be problem-solvers who are able to navigate the challenges of the twenty-first century requires more than just a "can do" attitude. High-impact educators are purposeful in engaging students in problem solving processes and strategies. Students noted that they regularly applied trusted processes such as looking for patterns, seeking evidence, or building on prior skills.

Even when they find themselves in unchartered territory, these systems, as well as bridging back to what they know and their repeated application, give them the confidence to navigate new concepts as they consider relevance, similarities, differences, credibility, and options.

3. What Else Should I Be Learning to Help Me Become More Effective?

Equally as important as considering what they already know is making a habit of taking inventory of what they need to find out. None of the interviewees coasted through college so prepared that feeling overwhelmed or unworthy were foreign to them. Despite the challenges they faced, many of those interviewed for this book demonstrated remarkable initiative to learn even when they felt inadequate.

Graduates figured out quickly how detrimental it is to ignore or hide their gaps. While some collaborative learners habitually reached out for assistance (often to teachers or professors, tutors, classmates, or colleagues), others dug into resources such as reading and videos with the needed determination to deepen their learning.

A recently-hired graduate working in commercial real estate shared his experience with online classes.

> I took an online course from (the university) for my realtor's license. You had three tries for the license and then you failed. Everything was online, reading, tests, everything. I tried hard; I was constantly online trying to make sense of it all but it was a terrible experience. So, I failed and lost my tuition.

After failing online, he decided to take the course from a face-to-face instructor.

> It was taught by a realtor who explained things, brought in real life examples. . . . I enjoyed the course and I aced the test. It was then I figured out that I learn best from discussion, seeing visuals, hearing examples, watching videos and asking questions. So even if a professor didn't teach that way, if they would take the time outside of class to answer my questions, then I could learn it the way that worked for me.

When participants grew aware of how they best learn, they became more purposeful in how they processed and supplemented learning, even when—or perhaps especially when—they did not favor the teaching methods.

As graduates talked about problem-solving, it was evident that they had reflected on it regularly and leveraged its capacity by applying it to many situations. This is what problem-solvers do. They are not born with some innate ability to "see" what others cannot or with magical answers no one else could summon. They learned, they applied what they learned, and it drove them to learn more. Impressive thinking and problem-solving are the result of consistently focusing on student growth.

WHAT PARTICIPANTS SHARED

Every college class is an AP course. —Freshman

The researchers for this book heard scores of comments like the quote above. Nearly every college freshman interviewed emphasized the difference between high school coursework and expectations versus the realities confronting them, just a few months later, as college students.

College seniors were more reflective. Instead of marveling at what had changed regarding the demands of scholarship, seniors in college discussed with the authors the changes within them and what it took to thrive as a college student, and frequently what they suspected would be a necessity to excel in their soon-to-be careers or graduate programs.

What changes are made for freshmen in college to succeed? What is required for college seniors to thrive in the collegiate arena as they prepare for their careers? At the core of the responses the researchers collected, the "work" associated with student growth boiled down to the critical skill of thinking combined with the agency to address challenges and problems. Successful college students and recently employed college graduates have separated themselves by, among other things, the following:

1. *Learning to think.* Learning to think is not the same as remembering information to recall for quizzes and tests. One after another, participants detailed the unique challenges they confronted with college academics. Perhaps unlike their K–12 experiences, their instructors assumed they would read the assigned pages and take steps necessary to remember the highlights. The thinking came when the student was asked to compare and contrast, via a five-page paper, the major tenets of last week's 40-page reading assignment to those of this week's 50-page reading assignment with the class discussion of the topics coming after the homework is due—not before.

2. *Disciplining themselves to think.* Thinking critically is not easy, and nearly all of those interviewed for this book indicated that it took some time for them to realize that "getting something done is not the same thing as thinking and learning—then getting it done." Therefore, when academics or managing a busy schedule or enduring sticky social situations become taxing, successful college students move through the difficult time because they have disciplined themselves to be critical thinkers.

3. *Making critical thinking a habit.* This newfound discipline, therefore, becomes habitual. Instead of whining about difficult professors, complicated assignments, and a less-than-ideal roommate situation, successful college students have made it their practice to navigate a way to success. If it sounds like adulthood, it should. The

most successful students, either only months or a few years removed from high school, have learned, often by trial and error, to think for themselves even when it would be easier to ask someone else to think for them instead.

College curriculum contains difficult content requiring more than an ability to memorize and recite. Participants shared that what they initially feared about academics in college was actually the easiest aspect to master. As it turns out, being prepared for a lecture hall course while being one of over one hundred students is straightforward: Show up. Pay attention. Take notes. Study notes. Take test. Repeat.

The real work, according to many participants, consists of learning how to "evaluate information," and how to prepare to "participate in a class discussion without sounding like an idiot." This requires showing up, reading, taking notes, studying, and a great deal of critical thinking.

Those interviewed for this book did not belittle memorization (knowing information is essential to the application of knowledge); they simply did not reference it as anything related to their growth. In contrast, their experiences with forming ideas and inferences, sharing them, and thoughtfully supporting them required a level of thinking that demanded their effort, practice, and courage.

WHAT IT MEANS FOR US

The most successful college students have been taught how to think critically. This may or may not seem obvious to educators, yet we cannot assume that all students are guaranteed to be equipped with the critical thinking skills required to accomplish impressive feats after high school. Not everyone survives college long enough to overcome an inability to think critically.

Furthermore, the relationship between critical thinking and success is not reserved only for those headed to the university. College is not for everyone, we know, for our communities are loaded with talented individuals contributing measurelessly without higher education experience. Significant adult contribution is difficult to provide without the byproduct of critical thinking, however. We know this.

A college education is not needed to be a critical thinker. We know this, too. The authors of this book chose to interview college students and recent college graduates. The authors, moreover, are confident many of the qualities aligned with college students' success also apply to those who entered the workforce directly after high school. Success is success.

Inexplicably, we too often fail to emphasize critical thinking during the actual class periods of K–12 education. This is when and where we fear the challenges that critical thinking creates. Instead, we can be tempted to teach what is easy to master and assess.

High-impact K–12 and college educators recognize the need to teach critical thinking despite its complexity. Learning to think critically is messy; sometimes students miss the mark, and their teachers are charged with being available outside of class and often reteaching the art and essential discipline of thought.

The mess makes it easy for us to, instead, choose a method of distributing clean information and periodically checking to see if our students can reproduce it for a grade. Our students can earn impressive GPAs and class rankings via this methodology, yet without the ability to think critically and apply learning, they are often exposed at the next level for what they cannot do.

Successful college students define themselves not by marching in an academic line and checking off their points earned to assure themselves of an A. They are organized, of course, and with that trait comes an ability to complete work on time and in a form deemed acceptable by their professors. This should be expected of college students, however.

The successful students interviewed for this book separate themselves because they are capable of participating with the curriculum beyond the simple completion of assignments and assessments. Their passion for their growth and their initiative to continue growing are palpable.

Top-tier college students can read a text and talk about it the next day in class without requiring others to interpret for them. They are not afraid to have an opinion about course content and do not struggle connecting the studied material to their own experiences when necessary.

These students view major paper rubric requirements as guidelines, if not limitations, not a blueprint for an A. They sometimes disagree with what is presented in class, yet they are capable of considering other perspectives and recognizing their own flawed reasoning. In essence, these students are critical thinkers.

How can we generate more top-tier students? Our students deserve the opportunity to create a product (a paper, a speech, or a prototype, for example) and receive rich, prompt, critical feedback about subjective assignments. But what if the student struggles? What if the assignment is completely awful?

This is the opportunity high-impact educators take to teach students something they will not forget. This is the moment that separates high-impact educators; anyone can give a student a checklist and hold her hand while she completes a fool-proof task. With this, high-impact educators are not content to end with knowledge acquisition. Despite the mess, discomfort, and necessary time, they venture with their students out of the comfort zone to apply knowledge, skills, and critical thinking.

We owe it to our students to ask more questions without definite answers, for within this grey area exists a student's ability to make connections not immediately apparent. It is incredible what can happen in a young person's mind when one of three questions is asked of her with an expectation of critical thought:

- Why?
- Why not?
- What if?

CLOSING PERSPECTIVE

A woman uses Facebook to tout a political opinion, perhaps urging others to vote for her favorite party and politician. A man reading this Facebook post, instead of ignoring it and moving on with his life, opts instead to reply with, "Why the hell should any of us care what you think about politics?" The original author officially ends whatever relationship could have existed with, "Why the hell do any of us care to read which concert you have attended lately?"

A referee makes a close call during a Saturday-morning YMCA game involving fourth-grade boys, and a disappointed dad questions the man's sobriety loud enough for every adult and child in the gymnasium to hear. While many parents are aghast at the outburst and ashamed of the man's behavior, a few others have awakened to the stimuli, almost instinctively, and see it as a chance to contribute their own mindless jabs at the volunteer referee. Again, loud enough to be heard in the adjacent YMCA pool, they question the referee's basketball experience, his physical fitness, and whether or not he is related to any of the kids playing.

In 2020, the midst of a new virus outbreak, citizens called for the government to step in and protect consumers from con artists selling fake medications to prevent or cure the virus. Despite consistent messages from the Centers for Disease Control that there was currently no known cure and that a vaccine was, at best, months away, large numbers of adults fell prey to scammers peddling miracle remedies.

Are adults incapable of determining what information is trustworthy? What are they thinking spending their hard-earned money on blatantly bogus remedies? What is the woman on Facebook thinking to post opinions about politicians she has never met to her online "friends," and what, exactly, causes the man to respond as he does? And what of the dad at the youth basketball game who opts to take after a volunteer official for missing a call? And his mob-minded minions, what are they thinking?

They are not thinking, and that is the point. We need only a few minutes on social media, a short discussion on partisan politics, attendance at a youth sporting event, or really anything else capable of stirring emotions to be reminded that not all adults show themselves as self-aware critical thinkers. In fact, the absence of discipline, decency, and reflection, all byproducts of critical thinking, have become commonplace, nearly a norm in some corridors of society.

Can age-appropriate thinking skills be *taught*, or is this quality simply *learned?* That is, were the respectful, reasonable adults at the youth basketball game educated to pause and think before they say something insipid, or have they simply benefited from superior DNA, some lottery winning that keeps them from frequently sounding like the fool in a terrible sitcom? With this, do lessons of thinking taught in school translate to the world outside of academia?

This is debatable, of course. We may know of people who have no viable excuse to behave like buffoons when emotions run hot; they had thoughtful parents, they went to college, they have good jobs, and so forth. Yet, there they are—screaming at some volunteer dad because he failed to call traveling on a kid with barely enough athletic ability to fasten his seatbelt on the drive to the Y. The origins of critical thinking are slippery, but what is not open for debate is the following:

1. The successful college students interviewed for this book referenced over and over their ability to think critically as a "separator" between themselves and those who have not progressed as far.
2. With this data in hand, and knowing its significance, high-impact educators owe it to students at all levels to place them frequently in positions requiring age-appropriate thinking skills and multiple opportunities to evaluate and consider perspectives beyond their own.
3. Educators at all levels know the importance of conveying clear and transparent learning targets. High-impact educators go beyond writing "I can" statements on the board and listing objectives on the syllabus. Students who understand *why* the learning is important are better able to exert the motivation, effort, and focus necessary to cement learning in a way that works for them and apply it to broader contexts.
4. Newly hired college graduates emphatically reference high-impact educators who go beyond memorization to facilitate application of knowledge, challenge them to think critically, and foster authentic problem-solving within and beyond the classroom as those who were most significant in preparing them for the challenges of the workplace.
5. Finally, high-impact educators must have the courage and relationship skills necessary to provide feedback for impressive and faulty thinking skills.

FOUR

Curiosity and Creativity

THE FALLACY OF CREATIVITY

Educational partnerships have grown to include a chorus of voices invested in the development of our youth. While there is a growing list of venture capitalists focused equally on disrupting education and collecting a hefty profit, many philanthropists are altruistic in their interest in promoting specific educational practices and outcomes to benefit youth and the job market.

Education-related organizations—including Kaplan, Knowledge Works, the National Education Association Foundation, Nova Labs, Educational Testing Service, and Pearson Education (to name a few)—have teamed with business powerhouses—including IBM, Exxon Mobile, Apple, Ford, Target, Microsoft, and Cisco Systems. These unions have materialized with an effort to grow a thriving global society, generations of graduates possessing an ample supply of the "Four Cs"—critical thinking, communication, collaboration, and creativity.

People with these skills, we have noticed, do well for themselves—and make Ford, Microsoft, Dell, and Cisco better, too. Indeed, it is in our best interest that those we educate prove capable of critically thinking (chapter 3), effectively communicating (chapter 7), collaborating (chapter 5), and, of course, displaying powerful creativity.

Creativity, however, has proven to be a resistant riddle for educators and educational partners alike. We love creativity, we say. The best among us, whether teachers or lawyers or software engineers, prove themselves to possess what many scholars and philosophers claim to be the highest form of learning—creativity. They bring into existence that which others had not imagined before. They cause things to happen, things others either could not or would not bring to fruition. They build while others are looking for the light switch. They create.

The researchers for this book interviewed scores of college students and college graduates (successful students by definition) with unique, often extraordinary creativity. These participants spoke about newfound abilities to complete tasks like studying, writing papers, and navigating the school–work–social life maze before them. Many shared stories about solving problems in new ways, both academic and beyond. All of those interviewed for this book emphasized in one way or another that they have learned to change the way they think in order to succeed. This is the essence of creativity. Ironically, few if any participants labeled their ability to generate fresh ideas as creative. When it becomes habit, it does not feel like creativity—it is what we have become.

But how? What causes some people to use their creativity consistently and powerfully enough to make business leaders team with school administrators across the country with the hope of producing more productive creators? With this, what stops others from impressively and consistently exercising their creativity? Further, is there anything we can do to ignite, channel, encourage, or teach creativity, or is it something some people own naturally while others go without?

WHAT PARTICIPANTS SHARED

Jumping through hoops is the biggest disappointment of school.
—College senior

Creative people have not attended special seminars on "How to Make a Masterpiece." Not one of those interviewed for this book, furthermore, referenced an isolated moment of magic within their youth that opened the gates of incredible creativity. Moreover, no participants fell out of bed one day capable of seeing a new way to manage a debt-to-income ratio or conduct a 75-member choir or organize the nurses' station to better meet the needs of patients and employees or design a virtual experience that would make riding a stationary bike bearable.

No special potions, no divine accidents, no lucky coincidences—just the result of high-impact educators teaching what is necessary to learn before creativity becomes a reliability. No, creative people have not been taught to be creative. They have been taught to be curious.

Becoming sufficiently and impressively curious takes time and discipline, and most students will not come by these naturally. The students and graduates interviewed for this book credit their best teachers for insisting on continual growth, for the creativity that Microsoft, Ford, Apple, and Exxon want from the generations to come is not rooted in a shortcut. The desire to know and to deliberate new connections and new ways of doing things is rooted in curiosity and nurtured by frequent interactions with teachers and parents who take the time to ask intriguing and meaningful questions, as opposed to simply giving information and answers.

When nurtured through exploration and questioning, curiosity powers the brain's capacity to build neural networks and synapses that form a wide net for capturing new learning. The more comprehensive the network, the more information and concepts will stick and grow exponentially with new experiences. The rigor of college coursework demands strong foundations of knowledge for all learners. Teaching strategies such as succinct direct instruction followed by active inquiry and engagement balance over-teaching and under-teaching and broaden both knowledge and curiosity.

The more learners know, the more curious they are. Over time, this reciprocal relationship builds creative thinkers who quickly set themselves apart from their less curious peers when it comes to problem-solving, innovation, and thinking outside the box.

While the authors of this book spoke with college students and recent college graduates to further understand how we should teach in order to prepare graduates with the needed knowledge, skills, and dispositions to thrive, two themes with a connection to creativity emerged from interviewed participants:

1. The Best College Students Are Inquisitive

The most impressive among our interviewed participants, those who spoke with genuine adult perspective and reflection, maintain a permanent, diligent relationship with their education. Whereas many around them view school as a series of tests, both literal and metaphysical, the most successful students have evolved to approach education as, quite simply, the opportunity (and necessity) to learn.

The result of learning may very well result in good grades for these students; in fact, it often does. Interestingly, many of those interviewed (especially college seniors and recent college graduates) neglected to reference good grades as either part of the process or even a desired outcome of taking classes. For these students, learning is its own reward.

One student, a senior nursing student, wasted no time responding to a question regarding what has discouraged her most as a student. "What has frustrated me? Jumping through hoops is the biggest disappointment." She added that, for her, it is no longer about *A*s and *B*s; that game finished a long time ago. She now learns for different reasons.

First, she knows that she needs to learn the curriculum, connected to her future livelihood in most cases, in order to be prepared for what is next—whether this involves a class, an internship, or the NCLEX (the test used to determine if she is knowledgeable and capable of becoming an entry-level nurse).

Next, she strives to learn because having knowledge has made her more successful, more powerful. Failing to learn—or not having an opportunity to learn—scares her far more than a poor grade could ever pretend. Lastly, and most telling, she learns because it is now who she is. She wants to know how, she wants to know why, and she finds joy wondering, "What if?"

"Jumping through hoops" is academic torture for inquisitive students; it is, for our most curious and talented students, akin to asking Wolfgang Puck to spend his time every day folding the aprons with a kitchen full of potential ten steps away. Moreover, hoop-jumping—enduring an elaborate, overly complicated set of procedures in order to, at best, prove comprehension of a simple objective likely mastered in the distant past—is counterproductive in reinforcing the need for our students to exercise their curiosity/inquisitiveness.

Creativity does not grow from closed-ended questions, hoop-jumping, or siloed learning taught in a vacuum in preparation for a test. The authors of this book found that the best college students have transitioned from prioritizing grades. These students and recent graduates want to know how, why, and what if. They yearn to apply their knowledge to the next phase of learning. They love to apply what they have learned to new and exciting puzzles. Whether they label it as such or not, they create. These students are not only the most successful but also the most fulfilled.

2. Successful College Students Want and Need Quality F eedback, Whether Face-to-Face or Electronic, from Their Teachers

Students may not know that feedback leads to inquisitiveness and that inquisitiveness is the fountain of creativity. They do know, however, that excellent, specific feedback from teachers is required for them to perform better in both their current classes and their future coursework. When students are given opportunities to conference with teachers and peers about their work to give and get feedback early in the learning process, creative processes and products can flourish. Excellent, specific, early feedback, especially when presented in the form of a question, is the most effective tool high-impact educators use to help students develop a strong sense of curiosity to initiate and grow their creativity.

According to interviewed participants, excellent and specific feedback includes what was done well within an assignment or a task, what could be improved, and an opportunity for continued learning on how that correction should or could be made. Successful students at the university level have learned that they need to improve as scholars, that they need to evolve. This requires rich feedback from their instructors, more than the acknowledgment that a task has been completed. As one interviewed participant shared: "A score is not enough—even if it is a great score."

This rich feedback is used so that the successful student can move forward. Those interviewed for this book appreciate connectedness between and among the courses they take. They expect to benefit from their classes both by the course itself being worthwhile and by it playing a role in the learning for future coursework.

How does feedback work, according to these participants? Successful college students learn by making connections between new content and what they have already learned. This is how we all learn. Top-tier college students are those who have grown to realize that failing to learn what is before them right here, right now, equals a significant struggle to learn what is coming next. Rich, impactful feedback can turn mistakes into powerful learning. When asked directly what the best, most high-impact educators do, more than a handful of college students and recent college graduates responded with, "They give the best feedback."

We do not create without first learning, and we do not learn without an understanding of what we do well, where we are missing something, and how, exactly, we can correct what needs correcting. Many of those interviewed for this book indicated that their desire for purposeful feedback came later in life (in college, typically) after being either uninterested or bothered by it as younger students. Interestingly, these were often the same interviewees who expressed profound gratitude for "those teachers" who insisted, via consistent and purposeful feedback, that they can and will live up to their capabilities.

WHAT IT MEANS FOR US

The Purpose of Grades

Most educators know enough not to be proud of growthless assignments, those aimed at taking up students' time and, perhaps, serving to fill the time teachers have in the classroom setting. Nonetheless, "jumping through hoops" happens in some settings, it seems, because the work gets completed by most students. Why? There are points attached, and grades matter to most students.

High-impact educators, however, know that points and grades are, at best, a decent reflection of what students know and how diligently they have worked to earn the points or a grade. At worst, grades are a letter or a number assigned to student work or performance before they were given the opportunity to make adjustments stemming from what they have learned—or not yet learned.

The best students absolutely do use grades as motivation. Yet these successful students (such as those interviewed for this book) take the most pride in earning high marks in challenging coursework that required growth (and perhaps even a little failure) via attending class, appropriately participating, working diligently on purposeful assignments and projects, and taking exams or creating products that require an amalgamation of their scholarly efforts.

Earning an *A* by showing up and completing an assignment here and there, receiving no feedback on the work, and subsequently seldom or never being challenged to process, rethink, apply, or evolve? Not only are successful college students not proud of this, but they also resent it to no end. Jumping through hoops hurts all students, and the best students know it. And creativity? If it is occurring at all, it is not because of the pursuit of points and grades.

Student Inquisitiveness

Creativity derives from healthy student inquisitiveness, and this reality should move up the list of our teacher goals. Teaching students to be inquisitive is not about turning students loose and hoping they explore their way to productive curiosity. This is aimless, often damaging teaching—likely no more positively impactful than stacking one "hoop-jumping" assignment after another and expecting student growth. Authentic, productive curiosity comes from students simultaneously being asked to improve a product, assignment, paper, or the like while also caring a great deal about the relevance of what they are striving to improve. High-impact educators understand that an inquisitive nature comes from a desire to thoroughly understand what is being taught.

One of the most impressive, articulate interviews for this book was with a college senior named Andrea, who had come to the United States as a high school freshman when she was 14 years old. "I was born and raised in Cuba, and my parents left everything behind in Cuba for my sister and me to have a better life and get a good education." While attending high school in Miami, Florida, her greatest challenge was overcoming the language barrier.

"Miami has a lot of Latino students. Many of us were motivated and wanted to learn. I wanted to understand and do well. It was frustrating at first. Often, I didn't know what was going on in a lot of my classes, but I was determined to learn English. I'd stay after class to try to get feedback so I could get better. Most of my teachers would help me; they would be interested in giving me feedback and helping me do extra things to learn."

Andrea credits those teachers willing to give her extra feedback and help as the reason she made it to her senior year of college. "I needed that feedback. Some were not interested in helping me. . . . I'm sure they didn't mean to ignore me. . . . They were too busy. But, I'm so thankful for those who were there for me."

Andrea shared that she was initially put in Freshman Basic Math because she scored low on the placement exam. "My 9th-grade math teacher, Mr. Briel, saw that I knew the content but not the language, so he requested I be placed in his honors class. He believed in me. I still go back and visit him every year."

As a college student, Andrea was used to working thirty to forty hours a week to cover her expenses but still found the time to continue to seek feedback from her professors to keep learning and improving in English.

> I've had to work hard in school, but I want to use professional words in both my languages so that I can provide bilingual services when I graduate. I keep working hard and learning from my professors' feedback, even when it's hard to hear because I know that language is power.

At the time of our interview, Andrea was set to graduate in less than two months with a major in psychology and human development. "I can't wait to begin working and helping people," she said, smiling. "It's my way of giving back to my parents and my high school teachers who believed in me. . . . They believed in me so I could believe in me, too."

High-impact teachers are willing to give students honest feedback and deliver it with the utmost confidence in their students' ability to grow from it. They are invested in student growth, and as a result, students are invested as well. Let's take high-impact math teachers as an example. They likely have students with impressive test scores. How? Do these instructors have a secret, advanced text no other teachers could find? Did they just get lucky and have all the smart kids assigned to their schedule? We know better. The best math teachers are impactful because the bulk of their students rise to their teachers' high expectations and unfaltering belief that they can reach them.

The students in a high-impact math teacher's class know better than to come to class without completed homework or mess around when she is explaining polynomials. These kids know that at any moment, they could be called on to answer a question. They know that somehow, someway, this woman will likely use every last drop of the fifty minutes designated for third period. These students know that bathroom breaks are better spent before or after class. The orthodontist appointment? No way, not during math class.

Cell phones? Falling asleep? Blurting out nonsense, thus distracting classmates? Making excuses for laziness? Blaming other people? Purposely disrespecting a peer or the instructor? Nope, not during math class. Students of high-impact educators know better than to try that junk.

Yet, remarkably, this math teacher is also adored by her students. Her students come to her classroom before and after school for help, and sometimes they do not even need the assistance. Student council representatives ask her to chaperone nearly every dance. Even struggling students, those who consistently fail to make positive connections with adults, somehow tolerate her. Is she a nag? Yes, but she nags respectfully and refuses to give up.

This high-impact educator also understands the significance of teaching complicated material to children and adolescents. She knows that not all students will flourish in math as she has, yet very few of them will forget what it meant to thrive in her class. Kids do not forget those lessons; they apply them to other parts of their lives. They use what they have learned, and they create.

High-impact educators, moreover, do not encourage curiosity and inquisitiveness by removing themselves from the learning equation—balance matters. Student-directed inquiry allows learners to explore their curiosity, but when teachers put too heavy an emphasis on it, they may fail to form the student's strong foundation of factual knowledge and belief in themselves necessary to learn high-level skills and drive deeper curiosity. Graduates identify high-impact educators as those who teach challenging curriculum and push students to understand it thoroughly and to the point of being curious about how it applies to past and future learning and beyond.

Reinventing Feedback

Based on interviewed participants' input, the single greatest divide between average and excellent educators is the ability and willingness to give correct, consistent, impactful feedback until student performance improves. Coupled with this feedback, the best educators conveyed absolute belief in the student's ability to improve his or her performance. A few defining truths are present within the feedback from high-impact educators.

To begin, high-impact educators are content experts. This is possibly forgotten at times within schools. As a premium has been placed on educators' relationship skills (and rightfully so), too often, students find themselves earning high marks in classes while receiving very little feedback from the teacher and demonstrating minimal growth. According to the college students interviewed for this book, this was often aligned with experiencing a classroom dynamic where standards were low, and the teacher could not consistently or reliably answer questions about the curriculum. Regardless of the relationship quality experienced in these courses, successful college students do not recall these teacher-student moments favorably.

Along with being content experts, high-impact educators are known for giving fewer assignments with more required student iterations. Students referenced authentic assignments that required a deeper dive and more learning per assignment. Those interviewed for this book often described what they called "meaningful assignments," the polar opposite of the universally despised "busy work" or the dreaded "jumping through hoops."

If creativity is born in curiosity, high-impact educators use feedback and student reflection as powerful levers, showing the student what or how something can be improved, why this iteration is necessary, and, most importantly, to what degree this newfound learning can be used in future scholarship, work, or life.

Based on what the authors of this book heard from college freshman, college seniors, and recent college graduates regarding what has led to their successes, a simple line of advice is offered to educational leaders at the K–12 or university level: reinvent feedback. If the work was worth completion, it was worth rich feedback.

CLOSING PERSPECTIVE

The successful college student mindset, as revealed in interviews with the authors of this book, includes the following questions:

1. What do I need to do to make this great?
2. What have I learned that can help me?
3. How can I apply it?

Application is where creativity begins. Creating something worthwhile requires student growth throughout the learning process. The curious student demands of himself that he learns, improves, and grows. From that, he can create.

FIVE

Collaboration

THE CAN'T-MISS SKILL?

Of all the twenty-first-century skills, including critical thinking (chapter 3), creativity (chapter 4), and communication (chapter 7), it is *collaboration* that has become a buzzword above and beyond the other desired aptitudes we hope our graduates possess. If we want our state-of-the-art professions to effectively produce, we need our employees, whether entry-level recent college graduates or senior management members, to function well together to achieve shared goals. This has become an accepted truth in the workforce. Further, it has become an expectation that educational institutions prioritize collaboration as a skill both high school and college graduates must own.

This expectation has resulted in K–12 schools and universities alike reimagining the process of educating students. With some outlier exceptions, the days of students sitting silently in desks while experts deliver curriculum are gone. Instead of the "sit and get" methodology, today's schools place value on students actively listening to their classmates and teacher, addressing and analyzing problems together, collectively brainstorming and researching to find solutions to problems, compromising when necessary, and working together to build consensus.

The payoff? We hope our graduates will be prepared for a world that has become so complex that collaboration in the workplace is no longer an option. We emphasize collaboration in schools not only to build these necessary collaborative skills but also because, when done well, it greatly assists in the learning process. As a result of collaborative learning experiences, graduates prove capable of owning a greater perspective (beyond that of the single teacher), an ability to see, understand, and empathize with a world outside of their silos. This results in a more successful class of graduates and more satisfied employers.

Collaboration in K–12 and university settings, however, has its challenges. Just as creativity (Chapter 4) is not realized by educators simply attempting to coax students to be creative or display their creativity, the act of collaborating in school does not necessarily and without a doubt result in (1) students learning more or more thoroughly, (2) students contributing appropriately, or (3) students undeniably benefitting from all collaborative efforts in that moment.

Everyone reading this book has suffered through a less-than-ideal, possibly even miserable, collaborative experience. Perhaps we recall working alongside the human bulldozer, the partner who, regardless of his or her range of capabilities, and regardless of others' capabilities, behaved as though everyone else in the group was too ill-equipped to contribute appropriately and ever-so desiring the human bulldozer to take over.

We may have experienced more than a fair share of collaborative zombies, those who, despite showing evidence of solid contribution in other areas of their personal lives, school, or work, inexplicably settle into a state of collaborative nothingness while allowing (or requiring) the living to do all the work. The human bulldozer and the zombie are merely two examples of multiple challenges identified by those interviewed for this book while describing productive collaboration.

It cannot be ignored that, first and foremost, students are individuals. This reality contains a tremendous weight for educators and educational leaders. A student's ability level? Individual. His or her preference for curriculum, content delivery methods, assignments, and the like? Individual. Readiness? Concerns? Strengths? Styles? The final grade? Individual.

Yet we know (or at least we think we know) that individuals benefit from a collaborative environment. Evidence validates this belief, and the interviewed participants for this book add to the evidence. *Successful* students grow from collaboration—sometimes even when the experience is either unpleasant or unproductive.

There is a vast difference between collaborating and collaborating well. Hearing from graduates about their most impactful learning proved to be valuable in understanding what good educators do. However, to specifically understand the impact of collaborative learning, the newly hired graduates were the platinum source for highlighting which collaborative experiences were most helpful and the nonnegotiable necessity of collaboration within their daily work.

WHAT PARTICIPANTS SHARED

> I know I benefitted from working with people, in groups, even when it
> didn't go well. —Recent college graduate

Interestingly, the interviewed participants for this book did not as a
whole describe their experiences with collaboration in the academic setting as being overwhelmingly positive. Many were quick to point out, in
fact, the potential challenges, such as surviving the human bulldozers
and zombies, associated with collaborating in school.

One college senior had a unique situation in which she was able to
compare the collaboration in her internship at a cardiac rehabilitation
program to the collaboration she was doing in her classes. "I understand
the importance of group work and its value . . . but it didn't always match
the assignment . . . like writing a collaborative paper."

She observed that peers tend not to hold others accountable. "We just
want to get it done. In the workplace that happens also—it really does—
some people do more, some do less, but in the workplace, we hold each
other more accountable. We are genuinely passionate about our mission
and work, so we are more likely to hold each [other] accountable."

Reflecting on a recent collaborative writing project, she observed the
lack of structure, expectations, and her perception that a group paper was
not a good collaborative assignment. "We were supposed to critique each
other's work, but we did not get any instruction on how to give good
feedback or how to build consensus, or how hold each other accountable. . . . It was more about getting the work done, regardless of quality."

In the end, among all three groups interviewed, more was shared
about the obstacles and disappointments than the benefits aligned with
school-based collaboration. Some of those interviewed enjoyed school-
based collaboration in the K–12 and university setting more than others.
Cassandra, a college senior majoring in marketing who was interning in
electronic healthcare, described a semester-long collaborative project in
her junior-level marketing class that was one of her most challenging and
valuable learning experiences.

> We partnered with a cupcake company and rebranded for them and
> presented it to them—all four groups presented to the company and
> the Dean of the school and our professor. We had a goal and had to
> figure out how to get it done. We agreed on the best ideas in our group
> and wanted to develop the best plan to share with the company. We
> pushed the extra mile to beat out the other groups.

Their hard work paid off.

> Our group won and we got some good feedback. One group had not
> put in the time, and it was clear. I can guarantee that it wouldn't hap-
> pen again. The owner gave great feedback, and it was apparent that she
> had some feedback that was real life. Not all of it was positive, but it

helped me grow, and it made me feel proud to work hard together and
be successful.

For some students, working collaboratively and engaging in small-
group discussion is how they learn best, and they shared that those experiences helped them process and make sense of new learning. For others,
especially college freshmen, collaborative learning provided an opportunity for them to get to know other students and forge relationships that
would not have been possible listening to a lecture.

In her freshman year of college, Emma reflected on the challenge of
being homesick during her first year. "I hated it here at first. I wanted to
leave so badly. In my 10:00 Philosophy class, we did a lot of group discussions and that's how I met two of my good friends. We started eating
lunch and studying together and just talking. That saved me. We still stay
in contact and get together."

Another student described transferring to campus as a sophomore
and feeling like everyone had already established friendships and connections. "Meeting people was hard. When we did group discussions in
class, those were some of the only times I talked to anyone all day."

Others shared that school-based collaboration was "a reality" but offered little more than that as a positive. Many bemoaned the stress of
being graded on someone else's work, even when the points were minor.
A fascinating aspect of that data is that every participant who spoke of
collaboration in school referenced it as valuable.

How is it possible that those who suffered through being marginal-
ized and minimalized in group work found it to be beneficial in the end?
How can the same results-driven graduate who lamented the fact that he
had, on multiple occasions, been forced to "take over" and do more than
his fair share of the work be the same person who shared, "I know I
benefitted from working with people, in groups, even when it didn't go
well"?

Yes, the best students, like those interviewed for this book (because
they have become college freshman, college seniors, and recent college
graduates), find a way to benefit from collaboration in the classroom —
even when it was painstaking. This is what the best students often do;
they overcome less-than-ideal circumstances and make it work for themselves.

School-based collaboration, it seems, is often experienced similarly to
a chore. Just as the dishes need to be washed, the bathrooms cleaned, the
driveway and sidewalk shoveled, and the yard mowed and raked, so it
goes with working with other people we did not choose as workmates.
We may not enjoy every aspect, but we eventually (in college or shortly
after college graduation, for example) realize it is necessary.

Perceiving a collaborative environment as "necessary" takes time for
many students. Highly skilled middle or high school students may scoff

at the thought of grouping with classmates to complete tasks or accomplish goals. Many at this stage of life see no need whatsoever to join a team aimed at a goal when working alone has proven to be both effective and far more time-efficient.

Yet one reality is clear according to those interviewed for this book: by the time a college graduate (typically the older versions of the same highly skilled middle or high school students) has begun his or her first professional position, everything has changed.

WHAT IT MEANS FOR US

It is no longer 1950. There is no smoking lounge in the faculty workrooms. Children with disabilities are no longer sent away to special schools. White-Out is no longer a necessity for typing long papers. With these, students are no longer expected to learn in school by sitting quietly in their desks for eight hours a day as their teachers provide curriculum in the form of lectures, notes, and exams.

Among countless other initiatives aligned with twenty-first-century educational practice, student collaboration in K–12 and most university arenas has become common if not the norm. With some glaring exceptions, "sit and get" is dead. Too many students were left behind sitting quietly in their desks as their teachers gave lectures, notes, and exams.

We learned that many students, perhaps most students, need more. They need to communicate during the educational process. They need to move while learning. They need to question new information. They need to discuss the curriculum content as it relates to their current abilities and connect it to what they already know. They need to collaborate.

Graduates are now entering a world where the knowledge they learn in school will not be enough. They must be prepared to apply knowledge while working and learning collaboratively to imagine and then reimagine ways to innovate, create, iterate, and solve problems. If we consider the highly technical and complex nature of today's jobs and the unparalleled rate of change within these jobs, it is not surprising that professionals find the need to collaborate to be successful.

Experts in business, technology, education, health care, engineering, and beyond point out the benefits of developing knowledge that is *T*-shaped. The top horizontal portion of the *T* represents a broad range of knowledge and skills, including the four Cs. High school graduates who complete their required classes should have a diverse base of general knowledge and skills, which they will broaden even more at the post-secondary level. However, unless they focused on an elective concentration, they do not yet have a specialization.

The vertical portion of the *T* represents deep expertise in the areas in which someone has extensive training, education, or experience. This specialization is usually developed at the post-secondary level and within one's chosen career. Both the horizontal and vertical portions of the *T* are important. Having a broad range of knowledge and skills, especially transferrable skills such as communication and collaboration, makes it easier to work with a wide array of people in different fields.

Having knowledge and skills that are both deep and wide is essential for innovative ideas and connections. For example, even someone with advanced skills in technology is not likely going to be able to develop an app to improve skills in crossword puzzles or guitar if he or she has never done crossword puzzles or played guitar. In addition, making those apps accessible to individuals with disabilities would require collaboration with specialists in education and health care. Educators are preparing graduates to enter fields that no longer work in isolation. The best educators have recognized the need for collaboration, including that which expands to cross-disciplinary partnerships. Those experiences were consistently cited by newly hired graduates as highly impactful.

Sean, a CPA who graduated with a degree in accounting, works as a tax consultant at a special-services firm helping Fortune 500 companies figure out how they can implement different initiatives to pay less tax. "In most of my classes, especially my leadership classes, we did a lot of group work. It's hard. . . . Not all do the work or contribute. But we balance opinions, and it was very valuable."

For Sean, seeing the value in collaboration in school became immediately apparent when he began working. "I am always working in teams. We work in teams of two to three and could be up to ten to fifteen. The problems we had with groups in high school and college are not unique. Here we have colleagues who put in so much and others who don't share ideas or put in as much work. . . . They are just there." The perspectives of Sean and other newly hired graduates shed light on three realities of collaboration. (1) Collaboration, even in professional settings, can be challenging, messy, and at times uncomfortable; (2) students need practice collaborating as well as instruction and feedback to do it effectively, and (3) collaboration in the professional setting is a necessity.

Sean described the importance of working with all kinds of colleagues. "I like working best with those who are interested in learning and have a good attitude and want to work here . . . but each team member is different, and you figure out how to work with everyone." As a high school student, Sean dreaded working in groups, mostly because he was shy. "Working in groups definitely took me out of my comfort zone. I didn't enjoy it at the time, but it was a valuable experience."

Effective collaboration in the academic setting has undeniable positive results. In an interview with Adam, a recently hired civil engineer who had described several collaborative educational experiences in college that were impactful, researchers asked him how much he engaged in collaboration in his current position.

"We collaborate all of the time," he responded, emphasizing the last three words. "Everything we do is done on teams. I do some tasks individually . . . those that I'm responsible for within the project, but we are always working collaboratively on projects."

Team members need to be driven and responsible in order for that teamwork to be effective, but they also need to be able to communicate and trust each other enough to ask for help. "If I get stuck, I can reach out to people on my team, especially the site design group. We have a broad group, and since I don't have as much experience, if I'm not sure about something, I ask."

Adam noted that even the engineers who had been with the firm a long time regularly consulted with team members.

> There's no way one person would know what is needed for every aspect of a project. We do a lot with underground utilities, water, storm sewers, and hydrology, where we look at land and figure out where water is flowing, then if we develop the land, we determine where we will reroute the water.

Each of his colleagues has specific roles and areas of expertise, but they work together frequently.

> I'm "Engineer One," so I do the design work, and all of my models are done on the computer. I'm responsible for entering the numbers, and they have to be exact. . . . If I'm not sure, I ask. For example, if it's a parking lot design, I have to collaborate with people on the concrete and asphalt design, grading, and creating a surface before the grading contractor builds the site.

Collaboration for Adam happened daily with people on his team, regularly with people from other teams, and even extended to people outside of his firm including clients, structural engineers, and architects.

The collaboration Adam described included learning newly emerged methods as well as expanding expertise. "Hydrology was an area I wasn't well prepared in. Ironically, it's 70 percent of what I do. I work with a great co-worker who is an 'Engineer Two.' He is three years into the job, and he specialized in it in college. I've been able to learn what I needed to learn from him."

Newly hired graduates working in a variety of professions reported that a significant benefit of good collaboration on the job was learning from colleagues who had more experience or deeper expertise in a specific area that they lacked. One recently hired graduate, Amanda, admitted that although she had a full year of technical writing in college, she did not see the class's relevance and put little effort into developing her skills.

> Now, I write reports all the time for management plans. . . . If I had known, I would have applied myself more to learn it well in college. When I first started doing my reports, my bosses marked them all up

with red and gave them back because they were way too wordy and long. I was super stressed out. One of my colleagues gave me copies of his reports so I could see what they should look like, and he would read mine over before I submitted them. I learned a lot from his feedback, and now I do them on my own and rarely get them back from my boss.

Caleb, an environmental engineer, described discovering within his first week of work that he was ill-prepared in the area of computer programming. "A lot of my professors had been out of engineering for a long time, and I don't think they used computers like we do now. We hardly used computers in our designs. It was mostly pen and paper—we don't do that at all now."

He described the college he attended as being dated: old buildings, classrooms that still had chalkboards. His description contrasted sharply with the sleek design of the firm and glass-walled board room of the building in which he worked.

> When I started working here, I had zero experience with some of the programs. I could tell two of my co-workers were surprised that I hadn't used some of the programs we use on a daily basis, so I would go in early . . . not clock in . . . and watch videos. If there was something in the video I didn't get, I'd ask our structural engineer or one of our geo-tech engineers when they got to the office, and then I'd go back to the videos until I learned it.

Caleb and Amanda's accounts of collaboration in the workplace fell under several themes that emerged from the research for this book, including technology, grit, growth mindset, relevance, feedback, self-efficacy, and communication. The researchers determined that it fit best under collaboration and reflected a stark difference between those still in college and those in the workplace.

Recently hired graduates recognized the benefit of learning from each other's strengths and experiences during collaboration, and they realized that they regularly needed to rely on each other to be successful. In the context of a high school or college class, that realization seemed to be, at best, an academic goal that did not always play out, even with the most authentic collaborative projects.

However, for many graduates in the field, it was a reality. Looking back, students still reported that they appreciated collaborative learning while in school. As professionals, they were grateful for what they had learned and were learning from their collaborative colleagues. Even though they were less than two years into their careers, newly hired graduates were eager to strengthen and support their colleagues as well.

Caleb concluded his account of the professors and programs that had failed to expose him to the necessary technology software programs by saying,

> My engineering program was seriously lacking in that area (*technology*), but people here helped me. Our firm just got brand new computer modeling software, and I was the first to learn it. . . . I played around with it and watched videos on it . . . basically read everything I could, and now I'm teaching people in my area how to use it.

His job experience speaks volumes about how, despite his chalk-wielding professors (or perhaps because of them), he did learn to collaborate, continue learning, and give back.

The results of collaboration in the academic setting hinge on one significant discrepancy; however, there is an astronomical difference between collaborating and effectively collaborating. High-impact educators know that having students work on a common task or activity, organizing them in small groups, and assuming cooperative behavior, interdependence, and individual responsibility and accountability guarantees one outcome alone—students work together with some classmates and apart from others.

Facilitating an academic environment with productive, purposeful collaboration requires as much planning and effort from high-impact educators as any other skill developed. In truth, high-impact educators do not assume that working in groups equates to collaboration—or superior academic growth.

Most students and recent graduates interviewed for this book, furthermore, did not share that collaboration in their K–12 or university settings played a significant role in their academic growth. Ironically, these same students and recent graduates spoke at length about the value of collaborating and how they benefitted from working with others in school. How does this make sense?

Perhaps the ultimate, most significant benefit of collaborating in school has little relevance to better learning English, math, science, or history. Instead, perhaps the benefit of collaboration in school is that collaboration itself is an essential skill, something to be developed if one hopes to thrive in the world outside of school.

Working with human bulldozers? Collaborative zombies? Struggle through meetings trying to survive the man or woman who is driven by an insatiable desire to share mindless anecdotes? A newly hired business finance graduate working in the mortgage industry recalled several examples of group members in high school and college whom he referred to as hitchhikers or poachers—those who are along for the ride and reaping the grades without taking any responsibility.

College freshmen and seniors had plenty of these anecdotes to share, but interviewing this enthusiastic young mortgage broker provided an opportunity to ask the follow-up question, "Have you experienced those behaviors from your colleagues when working collaboratively?" "Oh, all the time," he responded. Indeed, we have all experienced these pains, and most of us survive these collaborative meltdowns well enough to push forward and accomplish nonetheless.

Further, many of us have built collaborative skills enhancing our ability to benefit from and contribute to our groups and together create an impressive result. Perhaps having students experience the highs and lows of working collaboratively in school is reason enough for its emphasis. The interviewed participants seemed to believe this, for their comments could not make sense otherwise.

CLOSING PERSPECTIVE

High-impact educators do not teach English, math, science, or history courses and simply hope their students can write well, solve quadratic equations, calculate the force of gravity on an object, or explain why the United States uses an Electoral College. No, they teach in purposeful ways so that the curriculum is learned. Not much is left to hope in high-impact educators' learning environments.

Using collaboration in the classroom is no different for the most impactful teachers; it makes no sense to put students together and hope for effective, productive collaboration before first teaching them or having them reflect on that process and how it will be best utilized to benefit everyone's learning.

Some students interviewed for this book shared stories of poorly planned collaborative assignments where the project or paper is assigned, the students are grouped, and it goes from there. What happens? The driven students take over, and it gets done—and few enjoy the process.

Students did describe a variety of helpful strategies used by some of their teachers to facilitate collaborative group work. The following strategies were described by some students as being beneficial:

- assigning specific roles;
- setting expectations for collaboration (including listening);
- showing how to give feedback and how to build consensus;
- monitoring individual contributions;
- having authentic collaborative assignments (those likely to benefit from collaboration);
- utilizing planning templates;
- designating responsible parties;
- clarifying assessment criteria;
- providing honest feedback;
- factoring individual contributions and participation into grading;
- grading major portions individually;
- administering peer-assessments and self-assessments; and
- creating competition between groups.

The two strategies mentioned the most, especially by college seniors and newly hired graduates, were having groups set their own expectations and receiving honest feedback. When asked why it was helpful to set their expectations, follow-up responses referenced the value in students having "a say" in the process, forcing everyone to come to consensus on the process and commit to it, being able to use people's strengths, and "the process being clear."

While younger students may need guidance on setting expectations for group work, it is an opportunity to teach about effective collaboration. In addition, clarity is likely to increase for students when they set the expectations. Perhaps even more importantly, students, like many professionals, might be less resistant when they can have some ownership in the process.

When asked about the benefit of receiving honest feedback on collaborative projects, students referenced frequent check-ins by the teacher to ask questions and give suggestions that would increase the quality of work. In the case of collaborative project-based learning, the opportunity to receive feedback from a professional in the field was helpful. These strategies increased the group's quality of work, which they reported had a positive impact on their experience and learning.

Common among all of the instructional strategies (including expectations and feedback) utilized by teachers and professors was that despite describing them as being helpful, students consistently reported that several challenges still occurred within their groups. No magic bullet emerged that created a perfectly smooth collaboration that yielded maximum learning for everyone and a good time had by all.

Certainly, students must see a clear and meaningful purpose for collaborating, and at the very least, they should have a modicum of evidence of what each member can and will contribute; however, we cannot and should not expect educators to try to orchestrate perfect collaboration. Nor should educators avoid collaboration because of the potential drawbacks.

The goal of designing collaborative learning is not to remove every obstacle and challenge. Educators *and* students should be reminded that in all settings, including the workplace, it is in the messiness of collaboration and the convergence of diverse personalities and ideas that people learn how to collaborate. This is no excuse to continue practicing underwhelming, ineffective classroom collaboration, however.

When everyone in the group understands and appreciates what everyone else can contribute, is expected to contribute, and, in turn, does contribute, student collaboration can accomplish much more than merely providing some students with the experience of taking over when things go badly. Resolving conflicts, broadening perspectives, building consensus, and communicating with others are essential skills that should be taught and can only be practiced and developed through collaborative opportunities.

Our students all deserve the benefits connected to working collaboratively. That is not to say that students should collaborate 24/7. They need to be able to learn and work independently, but most jobs will require employees to work together. High-impact educators create opportunities to help prepare graduates to contribute to and benefit from professional collaboration, no matter the challenges.

SIX

Autonomy

"SMART ENOUGH" IS NOT ENOUGH

The authors of this book met and spoke with young people, ages 18–25, who were either in the beginning stages of their college careers, finishing their education, or new to the workforce post-college graduation. While many of these students and recent graduates spoke with a certain sense of arrival, as though they had crossed a bridge into the land of responsible adulthood, others seemed to be searching for it.

The differences between these two brands of participants were somehow both elusive and yet palpable. Interviewees consisted of youths from all walks of life, and these students and young professionals often possessed a combination of significant similarities and glaring differences with and from their contemporaries. The vast majority of those interviewed, for example, shared their ACT score and, regardless of the range, indicated that, for better or for worse, that score was a rather poor predictor of how they have performed in the university setting.

Interviewees included remarkably well-spoken (and vocabulary-rich) young women and men, sometimes expressing dissatisfaction about inaccurate assessments, their overall performance in the university setting, and being recognized and appreciated for their abilities. In some instances, they could not resist a temptation to route their scheduled interview into a modified therapy session, replete with examples of hardships such as unreasonable homework, finances, part-time work concerns, uncertainty, and keeping everything afloat while grinding for success in the college arena.

Other participants, often quite simpler with their words, seemed at peace with their current challenges (which also consisted of unpleasant homework, finances, jobs, and the challenges aligned with keeping all the balls in the air). In fact, many of these interviewed participants required coaxing to speak about themselves and their challenges at all—often focusing on their gratitude for those who helped them grow academically and as people, and excited for the careers for which they were preparing. None were exempt from the unforeseen challenges of college. However, those unfazed by the hurdles displayed rather remarkable outward thinking, including interest in the researchers' well-being, the study being conducted, safe and comfortable travels, and the like.

The authors do not judge the young people interviewed for this book. College students struggle with the uncertainty of a changing landscape, to be sure, and it is only fair to remember that the questions being asked of those interviewed were designed to bring forth truths. Succeeding in college and as a newly hired college graduate is not easy. Our participants conveyed that reality. Nevertheless, it became resoundingly evident that some students and beginning professionals are succeeding more than others.

The intellectual capabilities of those interviewed were based on information learned during the interview process (high school success, ACT, college GPA, course of study, speaking ability, and any other information reflecting one's intellectualism). What became readily and consistently apparent, however, was the reality that, given enough intellectual capacity to attend a college or university, "smart" was not the difference between happy, healthy, and thriving college students or recent college graduates and those struggling to move forward as students or professionals.

The most significant attributes of happy, healthy, and thriving college students and recent college graduates consist of the following characteristics of autonomy:

- *Self-awareness.* These participants spoke about who they are and who they are not, and they have made peace with those realities. They are purposeful about continuous improvement and mindful of their goals and priorities.
- *Self-advocacy.* These students and recent graduates seemingly had all the needs of their peers. Further, they shared how important it has been for them in their growth to advocate for themselves, seek help when needed, and stand up for what they believe.
- *Ownership.* The most successful participants spoke about the value of thinking independently and taking ownership for their decisions. Participants sought to decide for themselves as much as possible to avoid feeling helpless in the wake of others' decisions and, regardless of the result, owned their decisions and learned from them.
- *Self-efficacy.* The most successful participants spoke at length about the necessity of handling their own problems whenever possible—

because it makes it easier to handle future problems. Methods for solving problems varied significantly among students, but most striking among these participants was their confidence and steadfast application of trusted approaches to address obstacles large and small.

WHAT PARTICIPANTS SHARED

No one here does it for me.

—College freshman

The quote above was communicated in literally hundreds of ways throughout the interview process for this book. "No one here does it for me." This can have any one of a multitude of meanings. What is the "it" not being done for college students and recent college graduates?

This depends, of course. For some, "it" means reminders about when assignments are due. For others, it means doing laundry when necessary—and perhaps learning what *necessary* means. It can be paying for car insurance, remembering to complete the FAFSA every academic year, registering for coursework, navigating the obligations of a part-time job, or simply disciplining one's self enough to go to bed at a reasonable time in order to be a full participant in the 8:00 a.m. class the following morning. The "it" depends on the person, but every participant in this study had a list of "its."

This is where self-advocacy comes into play. The droves who spoke about their "its" have come to the realization (some much faster than others) that not only will no one oversee their lives and play the role of caretaker for them, but it is also quite unlikely anyone will step in to help (or know help is needed) unless a request for assistance is initiated by the person needing it. The college students and recent college graduates experiencing success boiled it down to this: to be successful, they needed to learn to do as much as they could possibly do, and they needed to know who and how to ask for help when that was not enough.

Many college students interviewed for this book gave a label for practicing self-advocacy: "adulting." Adulting, as they explained it, consists of the actions, behavior, and responsibilities required for success both in college and in life outside of school; it is the one-word description for possessing self-awareness, self-efficacy, problem-solving, and ownership.

Most adults do not describe their daily responsibilities as "adulting," for it is merely what becomes of us as we age and mature. A significant, if not overwhelming majority of college students, however, do not arrive on campuses as prepared, mature adults. They often arrive as children labeled as adults.

According to those interviewed, the earlier young people learn how to "adult," the more they will benefit from vital confidence and courage required to succeed as college students and newly employed college graduates. College readiness encompasses much more than academic readiness. "More than anything," one college senior shared, "I needed the confidence to know that everything's going to be okay."

Okay? Yes, a great deal of learning and embodying autonomy involves the delicate balancing act of knowing what must be addressed immediately and thoroughly (paying for the first semester before registering for second-semester courses, for example) and what should not consume one's life at the moment (such as having an apartment and roommates selected for a living arrangement two years in the future). From there, autonomous young adults can learn to appropriately confront one concern after another.

This is a trait of successful college students; they learn to prioritize because, as one college senior observed, "the little things will kill you if you let them." Fretting and obsessing over an unenviable parking spot on campus, the new smartphone one wants but does not yet have, and less-than-ideal partners for the group project assigned in Psych 101 will, according to the participants interviewed for this book, be the reason students prove incapable of rising to the occasion for the big things.

In encouraging and often humorous ways, those interviewed for this study shared that youths can and will overcome the challenges of transitioning from twelfth grade to the first year of college. When asked where he was least prepared when he entered his freshman year, Andrew, a college senior, shared that he did not have the skills to meet new people. He described his first semester of college as the loneliest time in his life.

> I grew up in a fairly small town, and I knew pretty much everyone and had a lot of friends, but I've always been on the shy side. My roommate was in sports, so he was gone all the time. . . . He was either at practice, traveling to games, or hanging out with his teammates. . . .
>
> He was a nice guy, but he was never there, so I literally spent every night sitting in my dorm room by myself. . . . I didn't know anyone.

By mid-October, Andrew called his parents, who lived in another state, to say that he needed to come home. His mom told him that he had to stick it out until the end of the semester, which was still two months away.

"It was terrible," he recalled.

> I knew I had to do something, or I wouldn't make it. One night I saw a bunch of guys hanging out in the room down the hall, and I recognized one of them from my math class. I grabbed my math textbook, walked down the hall, and knocked on the door and asked if anyone could help me with a math assignment. I didn't actually need help. . . . Math comes super easy for me, and it wasn't a hard class, but Matt, the guy from my class, stood up and said, 'Yeah, I'm in that class.' We started going through the questions, and after that, he and I and another guy

in the group always did our math homework together, and we started walking to class together and hanging out.

To this day, Matt is one of my best friends, and, needless to say, I didn't quit at semester break.

Sometimes self-awareness, self-advocacy, and problem-solving mean finding the nerve to knock on someone's dorm room and introduce yourself, especially when your parents will not let you come home.

Most young people venture into the college arena without the comforts of their recent past, including parents, friends, teachers, sports and activities. Although the question "In what areas were you most and least prepared when you started college?" was initially designed to highlight strengths and weaknesses in K–12 college academic preparation, there were often amusing revelations such as, "I had *no* idea that shampoo, laundry soap, deodorant, and stuff like that were so expensive. . . . I mean, I was kind of used to it just being there." Another student responded, "When my mom told me she wasn't filling out my FAFSA form. You know, she did it for me my senior year in high school, and then she just said, 'It's *your* turn.'"

Several freshmen admitted to finding out the hard way that even if the professor does not take attendance, going to class is necessary to earn a passing grade. They learned, some from the caring nudge of a professor and others from an automated academic warning letter from the Registrar, to evolve and develop the discipline to attend regularly and actively participate.

Looking back on his freshman year, Tyler said,

I knew how to study for an exam and take notes, but not how to take part in a class discussion. It was the end of my 3rd year before I knew how to do that well. Prior to that, I didn't feel empowered to participate in that sense, and in my senior year, I began to benefit from discussion and friendly debate.

When asked what led to that improvement, he replied,

Some of it was learning from mistakes and feedback . . . reflecting on what was and wasn't going well. We were expected to participate and were graded on our contributions to discussion, which made me realize that I needed to think about how I could *talk* about the reading and concepts. It was definitely an expectation.

Tyler also credited his campus work experience as a factor in strengthening his discourse.

I was working in admissions and supervising campus tours and programs. It involved connecting with people across campus, and as I trained others and began to redirect people, I was honing my skills. It eventually helped me benefit more from class discussions, but I wish I would have been ready way sooner.

Several factors, including candid feedback, authentic leadership experiences, and in-class learning experiences, contributed to his development. However, self-awareness and self-efficacy led him to acknowledge his gaps and focus on closing them.

At least to some extent, everyone leaves his or her parents and some or most friends. Everyone is exposed to new teachers, new academic expectations, and likely more rigor. Typically, most incoming college students experience an evolution in their participation in sports, clubs, activities, and involvement as a whole. College is different from high school, and mindfully evolving is a requirement for incoming freshmen.

The most challenging evolution to tackle? Autonomy. The interviewed participants shared that without the abilities of self-awareness, self-advocacy, ownership, and self-efficacy, no other talents prove relevant.

WHAT IT MEANS FOR US

To become autonomous, to diligently self-govern, we must first possess self-discipline—the willingness and ability to control our feelings and emotions to overcome weaknesses, and, despite temptations, attempt what is right. This is learned, and we should be teaching it better than we are. We owe it to our students to teach them, age-appropriately, what it means to be self-disciplined. Adult decisions require adult skills, and far too many interviewed for this book described either themselves or others as terribly lacking within this area.

How does this become an educator's job? Is it not the parents who should be teaching youths the necessity and benefits of self-discipline? Certainly, and the interviewed participants referenced their parents— along with siblings, aunts, uncles, and grandparents. Educators, in fact, can easily find themselves relegated to the backseat of a young person's life in comparison to the profound influence found within a family (see "A Note on Parents" following the final chapter).

Nevertheless, this research focused on the role education plays and has played in the success of children and young adults. Although good parents may know that graduating from high school is imperative and succeeding in college or the workforce is a blessing, they likely do not grasp the intimate inner workings of educational autonomy to the degree high-impact educators understand. We too often forget this. The authors of this book, for example, are confident knowing they should brush their teeth regularly with a soft toothbrush. One of the authors even flosses. This makes neither of them dentists.

Educational leaders know that K–12 schools and universities alike have evolved to address two undeniable needs: positive relationships and academic growth. No educator with a modicum of twenty-first-century realism will deny the importance of building and maintaining healthy, positive relationships with students while delivering a robust curriculum. We need relationships to motivate students and make the curriculum stick, and without relationship skills, high ACT scores and impressive GPAs will likely struggle for relevance.

The authors of this book address relationships in chapter 10. In short, relationships matter—more than we can even imagine. But what kind of relationship? Knowing students, knowing their passions, knowing their goals, knowing their fears, noticing and encouraging their healthy hobbies and interests, and being there for them are all necessary on many levels. However, if the relationships are not used to develop students as people and scholars to move them into a more capable future, we are not using our relationships effectively.

High-impact educators use their relationships with students to move them forward. They recognize and leverage the opportunities and teachable moments in schools that can play a role in the development of self-reflection and self-discipline leading toward adult autonomy. The following is a sampling of what must be considered for student growth leading toward college or career readiness:

- What are the expectations for the application of learning in class? What is expected for homework? Are there deadlines? What happens if deadlines are not met? What are the retake policies? What happens if students do not demonstrate proficiency or higher after learning and assessment have occurred?
- Are students encouraged to self-reflect and communicate with teachers about questions or concerns related to learning/academic growth? Is it required?
- What are the policies aligned with tardiness and absences? Is it okay to be late for class? What is missed when a student is absent?

High-impact educators, according to those interviewed, play a profound role, the lead role, in teaching youths and young adults to be autonomous by emphasizing the following:

1. Their students work to their highest level. Students interviewed for this book confirm what longstanding research has revealed about teacher expectations. Students are willing to work toward the highest expectations when they trust that their teacher believes in them and when they believe in their own efficacy to learn, even when it is hard, and even when it takes multiple attempts. Teachers who are focused on student growth create a classroom climate where learners are not afraid to fail forward and are willing to work hard, take academic risks, and focus on getting better, no matter where they began. Students who value growth and work diligently to-

ward continuous improvement mirror the expectations and values of their most impactful teachers.

2. Their students meet deadlines. Surprisingly, one of the most frequently referenced attributes that students cited as crucial to their success as college students or as newly hired graduates was their ability to meet deadlines. Many did not begin their college careers with the self-discipline and organizational skills to meet deadlines, but they spoke with remarkable honesty about the necessity of these qualities for success and for becoming the person they wanted to be. When discussing their friends who did not make it through to graduation, interviewees perceived that a lack of autonomy and discipline more than a lack of academic aptitude prevented them from earning their degrees. College seniors and newly hired college graduates reflected as far back as elementary school with gratitude to their teachers, including those who taught them tough lessons about punctuality and responsibility.

3. Their students are expected to solve problems, whether related to the curriculum or their lives. They are taught and expected to initiate conversations with teachers when they need assistance. The necessity of this habit will follow them for the rest of their scholarly lives and likely well beyond that. High-impact educators support and encourage students, but they resist the temptation to overlook or solve problems for them. When teachers are purposeful in developing learner agency, their students learn the enduring skills needed to solve problems within and outside the classroom.

4. Their students have learned the importance of time. Right here, right now. High-impact educators are not messing around. They establish their classrooms as the "right here, right now" opportunity that cannot be replicated. High-impact educators understand the potential of education to empower every learner, and eventually, so do their students. Time is not taken for granted. And if a student misses class? The student will be required to catch up—not for punishment, but because he or she missed something important. These standards may not make students happy in the moment, and it may appear as though a positive relationship could be hindered when expecting this level of growth. High-impact educators know this, and, quite frankly, they are not unnerved by the thought of bothering a student to work to his or her level, meet the deadlines aside from exceptional circumstances, learn to ask for help when needed, and use time appropriately. High-impact educators look at the relationship they have with students as lifelong; further, they know that with many students, the relationship will be viewed more fairly in ten years than it is now. Autonomy is learned. High-impact educators emphasize it.

CLOSING PERSPECTIVE

The most impressive participants for this study separated themselves from others on several fronts (communication skills, work ethic, and critical thinking, to name a few). Their capability of age-appropriate autonomy, furthermore, was an inescapable theme.

Perhaps not surprisingly, these successfully autonomous college students and recent college graduates spoke freely about their parents' role in developing this essential habit. They shared that, for their parents, being on time and attending with consistency is merely the recipe for mediocrity. The most successful among us—the decision-makers, the role models—separate themselves by using their time better than those around them. With this, they are as much as possible in control of their lives.

How do they do it? This seems to be the question we educators ask without careful consideration. Our mistake is that we often perceive students' self-discipline and autonomy skills as inherent with their upbringing. We know the honor roll students who play three sports, sing in the choir, and volunteer at the Humane Society were raised by parents who were not afraid to make their kids mow the lawn after soccer practice. All students deserve to be around significant adults who care enough to set high expectations in all domains and believe in their ability to meet them.

Educators focused on forming the whole person increase the likelihood of developing good people *and* accomplished students. Why would we resist? Do we think it amounts to luck? We know better. What are we teaching our students if they have three hours every evening available for television, video games, or smartphones? As the participants of this study shared over and over, conflict in college and the workforce is coming. Should we merely hope for the best when that time comes for our youths or be proactive and foster age-appropriate responsibility, benevolence, and autonomy?

The parents of our best students know very well why we should bother with aligning self-discipline and autonomy with our curriculum—because the value found within these lessons is endlessly more important than the temporary accomplishment of a high test score. All students, including and especially those who are not held to high expectations at home, need and deserve high expectations at school. Further, if students can "thrive" academically without putting in time, meeting deadlines, or asking questions, we should be wondering why we dare label it as success in the first place.

The majority of students interviewed for this book grew up with parents who created powerful, strong-minded children, who transitioned from the discipline of watchful eyes demanding that homework was completed, the lawn was mowed, the dishes cleaned, and the driveway shoveled to becoming powerful, strong-minded young adults, thriving in the college arena and workforce. Interestingly, these remarkable students referenced two groups of people they adore: their demanding parents and their demanding teachers.

"It feels good to feel like an adult," one college freshman said. Self-discipline. Autonomy. These are learned, and we should be teaching them. Many of those interviewed for this book lacked these skills and were forced to develop in a crucible of college stress, yet some do not—and they pay a tremendous price for attending a university with all the right test scores and not enough "adulting" skills.

SEVEN

Communication Skills

FIRST IMPRESSIONS

After the interview process for this study, the authors of this book scoured their data for educational truths. What leads to academic success? What holds scholars and the newly employed back? Most importantly, what can be done about these findings? Are there solutions for those who are struggling to thrive in the academic or professional communities?

Interviewed college freshmen, college seniors, and recent college graduates revealed several habits acting as sources of their successes and struggles. No habit is as brutally straightforward and immediately perceptible as the necessity to age-appropriately engage with those around us — to communicate effectively. The authors of this book were reminded early and often that appropriate presentation — how graduates carry themselves, their manners, listening skills, and ability to communicate with purpose — are essential for both short-term and long-term success.

Do they know how to professionally greet someone? Shake hands? Do they have a command of language? Do they speak with confidence? Are they friendly and respectful? How about nonverbal communication? Do they maintain eye contact? Do they appear approachable? Are they personable?

These abilities are not attained by good fortune. Young people *learn* how to carry themselves and communicate effectively. In a world filled with distractions and devices, they are *taught* these skills from the adults who know enough to model. Unfortunately for many, however, school may the only place where they have access to the modeling of well-spoken, professional adults. Many interviewed for this book lamented this reality — and expressed immeasurable gratitude for the high-impact educators who cared enough to model and teach communication skills befitting a successful college student or professional.

An odd dichotomy existed among those who spoke with the researchers of this book. Whereas every participant seemed to understand that first impressions matter (by outlining how important it is to "know how to talk," for example), only some of those interviewed, typically those quite advanced as scholars or as young professionals, made remarkable first impressions via their verbal and nonverbal communication skills. Interestingly, these were the same people who proved capable of best describing who, exactly, taught (or demanded) specific habits or skills aimed at making their first impression a great reflection of their capabilities.

WHAT PARTICIPANTS SHARED

The participants for this research referenced communication skills in multiple ways. Many reflected these skills and relied on them to separate themselves and open opportunities. Some were still growing in that area and were conscious of their progress, notable because of how much their communication had improved or because of how challenging but vital it was in their everyday lives.

Communication in all forms plays a vital role in helping students get to the finish line and is equally significant in the workplace. Jason, a recently-hired graduate, reflected on the role that communication has played in his job as a tax accountant. Jason went to a liberal arts college in Minnesota where most of his classes were smaller, and he had many opportunities to engage in interactive, open-ended discussions.

> Being in those smaller, deep discussions forced me to learn how to talk in front of people without being so nervous that I couldn't think. I was absolutely not comfortable talking in front of people when I started college. I still don't love it, but I'm more comfortable. The most important thing that helped me was to have an open environment where you are not afraid to ask questions . . . not afraid to ask a silly question or what you might perceive as a dumb question.

Jason shared that not only did it help prepare him to talk in front of clients, which he regularly does, but it has also enabled him to keep learning. "Tax law is constantly changing—you definitely can't rely on what you learned in college or studied preparing for the CPA exam." He noted that interpreting new law provisions is not always clear by simply reading the law.

> With tax knowledge, there's so much out there. To be able to hop in and have intelligent conversations is hard, but you have to talk to people to understand the parameters of the law. I go to coffee with mentors and managers and pick their brains about all kinds of topics.

> Reaching out and getting to know people and being interested in learning has been the most beneficial. For me, it is face to face interactions where I learn best. It was not always that way for me in college because it was so uncomfortable, but now it's completely flipped.

Students repeatedly referenced the necessity of becoming comfortable with those outside of their close circles in order to succeed in school or a new professional position. Further, they explained how the inability to do this hurt them in the past and how this inability caused some of their peers to struggle to the point of dropping out of college.

What does being "comfortable" with others mean? This is not some abstract euphemism or communal state of Zen. Being comfortable with others is the ability to communicate with them effectively. Moreover, success in college and the workforce is, according to college students and newly hired professionals, an uphill and possibly unmanageable battle without growth as a communicator.

When asked what became a necessity to succeed in college, the interviewed students bypassed answers like "to read faster" and "to study better." Typically, students read more in college than they read in high school. They study more, too. School is more difficult at the university level, and students who strive naturally dedicate more of their time and energy to activities such as reading and studying. Improvement in these areas is a natural side effect.

Unless impressive communication skills have been modeled, and the college student has invested in these habits, growth in this area will stagnate. Furthermore, even more apparent to college students and recent college graduates than their successful peers' abilities to read, write, calculate, study, or perform is the ability to speak effectively. The ability to fit within an impressive adult's world. The ability to get what is needed without resembling a child.

One college freshman, Sarah, described the panic she felt when she realized she had missed an event with her freshman mentor. She was part of a Future Leaders Club and had invited her mentor to an evening event the students had planned where all of the community and faculty mentors and mentees would have an opportunity to meet each other and participate in round table discussions.

> I was supposed to bring signs for all of the tables and moderate one of the discussions, but for some reason, the date totally slipped my mind. My mentor, Mrs. Davies, had young kids, and she had sacrificed an evening to go to the event, and I wasn't there. I was so embarrassed and mad at myself and didn't know what to do. People were asking me where I was, and I felt like everyone was mad at me and that I had let everyone down.

A few days later, Sarah sent an email to her mentor, saying that she could no longer be in the Future Leaders Club because she didn't have time.

> Mrs. Davies asked me to set up a meeting in her office, and we talked about what happened. I was crying and saying that I didn't deserve to be in FLC, and she shared about a time that she forgot something. We had a talk about keeping a planner and how I should have communicated when I realized I had forgotten. At the end of our meeting, she asked me what I had learned and said that what I did with that learning was most important. I learned a lot. I stayed in the Future Leaders [Club], and to this day, I'm still in contact with Mrs. Davies.

Those interviewed shared without hesitation what was needed to eliminate stress and thereon have more energy to dedicate toward impressive scholarship:

- "Where do I go to get a math tutor?"
- "Who is my financial aid contact person?"
- "How do I get a parking pass?"
- "What do I do if I have to miss a class?"
- "How does the work-study process work for me here?"

No, future college students do not need to know the step-by-step process of finding a math tutor before high school graduation. The minutia of everything involving financial aid need not be mastered in order to successfully and responsibly borrow money for tuition. What is needed, according to those interviewed for this book, is the ability to find answers, learn where to go for more clarity, or speak for one's self to get help.

"YOUR WRITING ISN'T BAD, BUT IT'S NOT GOOD—YET"

Students often referenced their initial surprise at the vast amount of writing their professors required—not just in English, but in almost every class. Acclimating to "high expectations" in their writing and thinking was a journey filled with a mix of humbling and encouraging feedback and *plenty* of practice opportunities. A college senior recalled reading his professor's final handwritten comment at the bottom of a paper that he described as covered in ink on every inch of white space. "Jacob, your writing isn't bad, but it's not good—yet." He didn't remember what grade he got on the paper, or examples of the technical feedback she left him, but he remembered the comment vividly. Laughing, he reflected, "I was shocked. My roommate told me that coming from Dr. Reinbold, it was a great compliment, which was funny, but it didn't feel like a compliment. I actually considered myself to be a good writer. It reminded me that I had work to do but that I could get better, and I did."

For college and university students, the power of communicating effectively carries its most considerable weight not in the ability to write a great essay or give a terrific presentation to conclude a group project (although these abilities matter), but instead in the practice of self-advocacy. Appropriate assertiveness via communication skills defined almost every college senior interviewed.

As for college freshman, some were beginning to recognize the importance of communicating effectively. Many were likely not yet forced into this realization, and it showed. It will happen before too long if they are to be college graduates. Successful college graduates learn to communicate as impressive adults because they learn that failing to do so results in being treated like a child.

Note of Interest

Not every college student and recent college graduate interviewed for this book spoke and behaved like an impressive adult. These were college kids, and many of them, for better or for worse, carried themselves and spoke like college kids. Truthfully, even a few of the newly employed recent college graduates who contributed to this research struggled to resemble a responsible adult when they participated. This takes more time for some, the authors know.

Nonetheless, a theme emerged from the gap between the communication skills "haves" and "have nots," and it speaks volumes. Nearly if not every participant who dwelled on negative experiences (defined by the authors as offering unsolicited grievances about personal life, the university, professors, peers, and so forth) with people or circumstances struggled significantly with their interpersonal and communication skills.

Those who described setbacks or conflicts as learning opportunities, however, had the most impressive interpersonal and communication skills. They displayed impressive self-advocacy. "Stuff happens with people sometimes," one college senior shared. "You just got to meet these people head-on, talk it out, and move forward. . . . Because you don't have time to get dragged down."

Self-advocacy with the inclusion of age-appropriate interpersonal and communication skills is conflict resolution at its purist. In this study, those who possessed these skills were well ahead of the pack. Those who spoke and behaved like children complained about being treated like children—and they subsequently struggled with issues their peers overcame months or years ago.

WHAT IT MEANS FOR US

Confident, successful adults are capable (if not comfortable) interacting with other adults, even if the interaction is stressful. Effective communication skills, it seems, are those that reach well beyond an enhanced vocabulary, a solid understanding of comma placements, or the ability to read sections of a text aloud.

These skills and many others associated with English and the other curricula are essential for students as they progress from childhood (grade 5, for example) into young adulthood (freshman in college). We cannot expect a freshman in college to thrive with a fifth-grader's vocabulary, reading ability, or writing skillset. And, as was unearthed in the research for this book, most successful college seniors cannot make the transitions they need if their academic communication skills have not substantially improved from their freshman year in college.

But it is more than this. Academic growth—such as reading ability, comprehension, vocabulary, grammar, and the like—is assumed for student growth. Unfortunately, however, too many highly capable, academically skilled youths are relegated to the sidelines during some of life's most demanding moments, not because they do not have the words, but because they cannot or will not use their words when the time calls for it.

The most successful students interviewed for this study—those with impressive accomplishments and unmistakably bright futures—spoke fluently and correctly, for the most part. None of them grunted double negatives while searching for their fifth-grade vocabulary. This was not what separated these young people, however.

They met the authors of this book as adults, as equals. They were confident—even when they did not know what to say. These young scholars and professionals had evolved out of the shield of childhood, where they spoke about fun and fancy while allowing adults to handle the important things. Even if they appeared as youth with their clothes and hair and interests, they handled their important things as adults.

Those skills, both academically based communication and self-advocacy, are learned. Participants, at length, praised those who taught them how to communicate and self-advocate:

1. Parents: Over and over, "my parents" was the answer to so many questions asking participants to share how they have grown to their current state.
2. High-impact educators: English language arts teachers? Of course, but no English teachers have enough time to teach the communication skills the most impressive of those interviewed for this study possessed. As the authors heard time and time again, many high-impact educators committed to the growth of these young people. They taught rigorous curriculum, and they expected personal

growth. They modeled elite communication skills and self-advocacy. They tirelessly recognized and utilized teachable moments.

Interestingly, the point of emphasis shared by the highly impressive participants was not merely that their parents and best teachers taught them or even what, specifically, the lessons on communication skills and self-advocacy were (the interviewed participants each had their own challenges and areas requiring emphasis), but instead that their parents and best teachers continually expected more from them than they were currently giving.

Great parents and high-impact educators, according to high-flying participants, would not allow stagnation, even if the child/student was already thriving. Their encouragement and belief that even if they had progressed from *not bad* to *good*—or even to *great*—they had not yet arrived at *their* best.

This reality explains the skillset of a twenty-two-year-old male participant, newly employed at a real estate company. He had recently graduated from college and agreed to meet the authors for an interview at his workplace. He was, in his words, "not a great student."

He did not speak with the Queen's English; his vocabulary was professional but plain. During the interview, he reused pet phrases such as "clutch performance," how a habit was his "go to," and how anything landing on truth deserved "fact." Without being present for the interview, scholars would be tempted to dismiss this young man as having significant lapses with his communication skills, undoubtedly hindering his professional future.

In fact, he was remarkable in his ability to communicate effectively. He met the authors at the business's entrance, escorted them to a comfortable conference room, provided them with amenities, and spoke with them with no hesitation of any sort. He knew he was their equal, and that made it so.

The plain language, the pet phrases—these disappeared behind a humble yet proud professional, a man who admitted, with a smile, where he needs to grow and what had helped him succeed as a student despite not being gifted with Winston Churchill's articulation.

His parents expected him to be impressive, so he has been. His best teachers expected more from him, so he worked harder. He learned how to "speak up," how to ask for what he needs. He learned that communicating like an impressive adult is not an exclusive designation for communication majors. He learned that he would never be finished learning how to better communicate. He is the product of great parents and a few incredible, high-impact educators.

WHAT HIGH-IMPACT EDUCATORS EMPHASIZE ABOUT THE IMPORTANCE OF COMMUNICATION SKILLS

High-impact educators were described by interviewed participants as being genuine, knowledgeable, and relentless in their expectations for students. The essential habit of possessing strong communication skills requires two distinct areas of growth: communication of content knowledge and the willingness and ability to use it.

Learning these does not happen because we hope for it. Interviewed participants assured that their ability to speak with knowledge, purpose, and confidence came as a result of their parents and these dogged educators never backing off. Specifically, high-impact educators:

- *never allow their students to believe that others can or should speak for them if they are capable of speaking for themselves.* "Why are you crying?" "What could you have said?" "Tell me what you do when your reading comprehension begins to falter." "What evidence can you offer to support that inference?" High-impact educators understand that the better their students' communication skills, the better their students' lives. College students do not drop out of college because they are stupid; they drop out of college because they fail to speak up before their problems become insurmountable. Young professionals do not miss out on career opportunities because they did not know the right people; they miss out because they struggle with how to speak to the people they need to know.

- *never allow their students to become victims of a situation if speaking up can correct the situation.* "What happened on the playground?" "What do you think the consequence should be?" "What do you want me to understand?" "Why are you struggling with the multiple-choice tests in Psychology 101?" "How could you write that idea more clearly?" High-impact educators know that silence can kill the spirit of youths and adults alike. Not knowing what words to use to express one's self is a prison sentence. Not having the confidence to use the words we have is no better. These skills are essential; without them, we are run over by people with lesser ideas.

- *insist that their students grow in character and confidence with an ability to self-advocate with age-appropriate communication skills.* In the eyes of a high-impact educator, no one ever arrives. We are all beautiful, we are all special, we all have amazing talents, and most importantly, we are not yet good enough. This is a hallmark of high-impact educators. They master the art of making students feel loved and appreciated while at the same time reminding them that there is work to be done if they plan on being special tomorrow. Coincidently, it takes truly incredible communication skills to teach young people the significance of communication skills.

CLOSING PERSPECTIVE

For a variety of reasons, young people often put a lot of energy into hiding their gaps. Perhaps we all do, at times. Our educational system has long focused on grades and mass achievement of standards at predetermined times. As a result, the uniqueness of learners is often obscured. Schools and colleges should be places where students can discover their strengths and passions. They must also be places where students can uncover where their knowledge and skills are lacking and have opportunities to learn and improve with the purposeful guidance of trusted educators.

Even in institutions filled with caring, attentive educators and systems of support, individual student gaps and struggles can go undetected, especially when students lack the communication skills or the self-efficacy to address them early on. The fear of looking stupid, not belonging, or being the only one in the room who does not know prevents some students from asking for help.

All educators have encountered students who are determined to cover that fear in perplexing ways such as pretending not to care, blaming the teacher, or giving in to any of the hundreds of tempting reasons to quit—the high cost of college, missing friends and family, living in meager living quarters, feeling stressed, failing a test, not feeling a sense of belonging, experiencing relationship break-ups, and tiring from the hard work and dedication required to keep up, to name a few.

It is not a question of *if* young people will need a safety net to overcome challenges, but *when*. They all need the support of people around at some point to help them get back up and keep them moving forward. The ability to communicate with those trusted sources of support and advocate for their needs was, for many interviewees, a lifeline to college success.

Educators cannot be expected to be clairvoyant in responding to student needs. Still, they increase their positive impact on all learners when they take the time to get to know students and open lines of communication. How a student responds to a failed test or a feeling of inadequacy is often dictated by the teacher's response. The most powerful indicators of an educator's teaching philosophy are seen in the micro-decisions made in the moment— in the midst of a class discussion, in response to a troubled expression, or on the return of an absent student. Educators and students each have the power to open entry points to get students on the right path, and each can just as quickly close them off.

At every developmental level, educators have the opportunity to teach communication skills in all forms. Communication can enhance learning in all content areas and is a skill that is necessary for the workplace. The students interviewed for this book shared that they did not always enjoy communicating in class. In fact, for many, the experience was outright uncomfortable. Nonetheless, at some point in their schooling, their teachers required it, and those who emphasized it were credited with helping graduates develop this essential life skill for continued learning and success.

Communication skills are learned from high-impact educators who embed communication into the curriculum and leverage every teachable moment to emphasize its importance. These skills serve students far beyond possessing a serviceable vocabulary and an impressive grasp of grammar, sentence structure, and writing as a whole—they also play a leading role in giving students the confidence to communicate, via the written or spoken word, when silence is not an option.

12 COMMUNICATION-RELATED PRACTICES OF HIGH-IMPACT EDUCATORS

1. High-impact educators teach communication skills in all forms— speaking, writing, listening, and dialogue.
2. High-impact educators build trusting, supportive relationships to open lines of communication.
3. High-impact educators know that the most impactful teaching opportunities are in their reactions and their proactive discussion about the role that gaps and mistakes—even failure— can have in healthy growth.
4. High-impact educators facilitate self-reflection and metacognition to help students monitor their learning and adjust before it is too late.
5. High-impact educators encourage students to communicate and advocate for their learning needs and teach them how to tap into resources and support systems.
6. High-impact educators model the belief that with effort and support, gaps in skills and knowledge can be significantly improved.
7. High-impact educators provide opportunities for ungraded practice, for students to learn from their mistakes, receive early feedback, and self-reflect.
8. High-impact educators respond when students come forward, admitting a gap.
9. High-impact educators check in with students early and often to help them identify needs and focus on closing gaps in their learning.

10. High-impact educators initiate conversations with students when they do not come forward, and they differentiate their instruction, especially when what they are teaching is essential and challenging.
11. High-impact educators know that *smart* is not one thing, and they help students use their strengths to improve in multiple areas.
12. High-impact educators know that it is never too late to learn, and they make sure that their students know this also.

EIGHT

Determination and the Growth Mindset

It's supposed to be hard. If it wasn't hard, everyone would do it. The hard is what makes it great. —Jimmy Dugan, *A League of Their Own*

"The hard is what makes it great." The seven-word sentence defines and embodies the growth mindset better than any sophisticated, academic attempt available. We value accomplishments that come at a steep price. We cherish the accomplishments that come after struggle, for we remember the struggle; we remember the pain or embarrassment or dissatisfaction or even the burning rage that accompanied falling short of the goal. This creates within us a determination, an insistence to carry on, however unpleasant it may be in the moment. Being better, having more, and reaping the rewards is hard. For some, it is too hard. For others, doing what is challenging becomes a habit.

What is the difference between these types of people as they relate to the growth mindset? One could argue that some people are simply gifted with more talent; therefore, they either have fewer struggles or more to offer in their fight against struggles. Perhaps, instead, some people are better "wired" for determination, as though a growth mindset is itself a form of unearned talent. Along with every hardworking person on Earth, researchers know that none of this is true. The most significant difference between a person with a tremendous growth mindset (perhaps the only difference) and someone struggling with "hard" is the ability and willingness to push through discomfort.

Discomfort. It is, perhaps, the single most effective enemy of accomplishment. People will remain in a current state, sometimes even within an unpleasant reality, because the change requires discomfort. Some people would love to quit smoking cigarettes but cannot. Some people know they need to take steps to stop drinking alcohol but cannot. Some people know they need to exercise and eat healthy but cannot.

And some people know they do not understand their math homework, know they are destined to miserably fail their next exam, know they should make arrangements to meet with Mrs. Heinert before school for help, know that they need to dedicate less time to their video games and more time to studying math, know that struggling in math is going to interfere with so many important goals (acceptance into and succeeding in college, for example), and know that the time to act is now—but they cannot.

If avoidance becomes a habit, we will sidestep "hard." For those with a growth mindset, however, working through difficulty becomes an accomplishment itself. These people are typically no more skilled than those around them. In fact, many of the most determined people are those who know all too well how feels to be less talented. Working hard did not begin as a pleasure for many who embody a growth mindset; they simply had to grind to get where they wanted to be.

And the goals? Do these people always accomplish what they set out to do or learn? Of course not, but the difference between the most determined among us and people who too frequently become paralyzed by the avoidance of discomfort is that determined people have come to believe (to know) that they win even when they fall short of their challenging goals. They have grown from the work; it gives them strength.

Talent is attractive. It glows. Hard work, however, lives in the gap between those who habitually accomplish impressive feats and those who have convinced themselves that aiming high is not worth the disappointment. Owning a growth mindset is having courage enough to work like mad at something while realizing that both discomfort and failure are part of the process.

Where is the growth mindset developed? Home and school. Great parents and high-impact educators instill the peerless habit of determination into their children and students. They recognize talent, of course, but they praise hard work—even and especially if it results in failure. They are called to make children stronger and more capable, for they know that most of the challenges ahead for these young people will happen when the parent or teacher is removed and thereby unable to solve the problem for the child or young adult.

WHAT PARTICIPANTS SHARED

> Those who are curious want to learn and work hard to get it. —College senior

Sometimes themes emerge from answers to seemingly benign questions. The authors of this book asked interviewed participants to discuss whether or not they believed their ACT/SAT scores were a reasonable predictor of their performance at the college or university level. As a reminder, the ACT and SAT are designed to measure college readiness and predict success in the first year of college.

The responses were overwhelmingly one-sided. In mass, college freshmen, college seniors, and recent college graduates did not believe their ACT or SAT scores predicted much of anything related to their higher education performance. What did? For many, especially those who described having teachers who challenged them, the high school GPA was actually a far more accurate predictor of college performance than was the ACT/SAT score.

The participants explained that the ACT/SAT was "one test, one day." Their high school GPA, however, was a reflection of their commitment and work ethic—whether they found their high school coursework challenging or not.

Tanis, who was in her senior year of college, had a 26 ACT score and a 4.0 GPA going into her last semester as a computer science major.

> I know people who are smarter than me but have low GPA's or had to drop out. Some really smart people don't make it because they are lazy, but most of the time it's because they aren't curious about learning, so they don't put in the effort. You can have all of the talent, but if you aren't curious about learning, you won't put in what it takes to learn at this level. If you are a hard worker, it will likely work out unless you really are not grasping the technical information. . . . Usually, however, those who are curious want to learn and work hard to get it.

Even participants who claimed their ACT/SAT scores were well above average (if not fantastic) shared this perspective. Yes, some tests mattered, the authors heard. Further, some courses of study (pre-med, for example) require heavy testing and impressive test scores. Nonetheless, these interviewees explained that their ability to be either brilliant or competent once a week in the form of test-taking may or may not be present and relevant in the moment, but it is most certainly irrelevant to their ability to succeed beyond school. Success, they offered, does not come from an impressive moment of testing; it comes from the work required to apply their knowledge or comprehension to that moment of testing—even if that moment does not turn out great.

This is why colleges and universities have countless struggling students who once nailed the ACT/SAT in high school while simultaneously being home for countless others who are thriving despite rather unimpressive ACT/SAT scores. Determination is the wildcard. With it, the average can make up for disadvantages, and the gifted can soar beyond belief. Without it, talent is lucky to see the light of genuine accomplishment.

It's more interesting when you're being challenged. —College senior

Every interviewed participant—literally every student and recent graduate—referenced his or her persistence as a major factor, if not the most
prevalent force, leading toward their successes in college. In particular,
students spoke about the following adjustments they quickly determined
necessary for collegiate life:

- improved study habits (limiting distractions, for example);
- studying longer (few students realize at first that being a college
  student is a full-time job);
- working more job hours (this is inevitable for so many, for college is
  expensive, and expenses do not wait);
- time management (successful scholars eventually learn to use more
  of their twenty-four hours);
- sacrifice (successful scholars learn that some things need to go
  when the goals are challenging); and
- focusing on short- and long-term goals (thriving college students
  knew the person they wanted to be, even if that formation was a
  work in progress).

Changing one's life to work harder while sleeping less and delaying fun
requires fierce determination from most young people. Most of those
interviewed indicated that they did not enter college with these habits.
Rather, they were forced to adjust their routines, often a great deal of
their lives, to simply survive in the college or university setting. Even
then, this survival did not necessarily equate to success for many students.

Insisting on Feedback

Many college students shared that, despite the combinations of studying more, sleeping less, and sacrificing creature-comforts and other
wants, their academic goals still proved to be elusive before taking even
more significant steps. These students, often describing the next steps as
acts of desperation, took their persistence to a new level by using it to
bolster communication (chapter 7) with their instructors and professors.

They outlined the process of dedicating time and energy to achieve
academically, only to face immense disappointment when either the
learning or the grade or both did not coincide with their effort. What
then? How does persistence and communication with professors translate into improved learning and grades? Consistent and productive dialogue with instructors leads to high-quality feedback. This feedback, the
participants explained, leads to improvement. High-impact educators, as
is emphasized throughout this book, naturally provide rich feedback.

Some teachers do not. Determined, persistent students demand it anyway.

A Growth Mindset

There are differences between college freshman and college seniors. They look different, of course, but there is so much more separating the two groups. Freshmen are kids learning how their talents and personalities best align with a course of study and, eventually, a career. Many are still wondering if they belong, or if their college careers will amount to nothing more than an attempt.

Freshmen, despite earnest efforts to discover what they want to do and who they want to become, are closer to high school pep rallies and prom than they are to signing a contract that includes vacation time and health insurance. The full picture of the kind of person they can be is still in formation. They are learning how to learn.

College seniors have chosen their route, and they are merely a few short weeks or months away from graduating into the formidable world of adulthood. They have chosen either careers to pursue or graduate degrees required for their future endeavors. They speak differently than they did a few short years earlier. They have new concerns, new worries, but they also have a sense of confidence and peace that is missing from nervous, naïve freshmen. They are closer to becoming the person that they know they can be. They have figured out how to become educated.

The difference between college freshman and college seniors, aside from age and time spent in school, is the presence of what has likely become a well-established growth mindset, a belief that significant accomplishment is achieved through dedication, hard work, and persistence—that IQ and other natural talents are merely a starting point. A growth mindset fosters dedication and a love of learning because it continuously rewards.

Working toward goals with dedication and persistence (growth mindset), students shared, leaves far fewer stones unturned than attempting to succeed with fewer, less thorough methodologies. Many freshmen struggle because their methods consist of studying with one counterproductive distraction present after another. Their high school careers survived this, they shared. College seniors evolve to protect themselves from these pitfalls. It must be noted—there are far fewer college seniors than there are college freshmen. Colleges and universities struggle to turn freshmen into sophomores.

Proud of Failure

Developing a growth mindset is delayed for many or most college students because dedication and persistence in the academic arena require failure. The interviewed participants spoke about "hitting a wall," the moment when being a successful student required more from them than was comprehensible in their past. Some hit their wall in elementary school, where it became evident that their reading ability was substandard. For others, the middle grades exposed significant math deficiencies. Almost every interviewed participant, furthermore, described a wall at the college level.

This is either where the students made adjustments, persisted, and found success, or where it became habitual to retreat from their failure and focus elsewhere. Successful college students have some skillsets stronger than others, of course—thank heavens there are different paths of study available. But altogether avoiding unpleasant curriculum content, less-than-ideal settings or instructors, or even classes offered at certain unfavorable times in order to tackle only what is comfortable, easy, or enjoyable is a debilitating formula for stagnancy.

When the interviewed college seniors were asked to explain why and how they progressed to the final stages of a college education while some of their peers did not, they gave several answers: their equally talented classmates lacked autonomy (chapter 6) and the ability to communicate their concerns (chapter 7), and, most glaringly, they did not know what do when things got "hard."

College is difficult for everyone, students shared. Some students have grown to possess impressive resiliency in the face of conflict and challenges, and some, unfortunately, have not. Every interviewed participant referenced personal failure. It was striking to hear the differences between those who were capable of describing what was done (or what is being done) to overcome it against those (usually freshmen) who, at least for the time being, appeared to have no plan for overcoming it.

WHAT IT MEANS FOR US

A Plan for Failure

If we hope for our students to succeed as they progress into adulthood, we absolutely must teach them to build and use determination and a growth mindset. To accomplish this, we must understand the value and opportunity available within failure. Whether or not we label or grade it, failure either is or soon will be experienced by every student.

This is good; it means we are pushing students as high-impact educators should. In fact, the longer our students wait to experience academic struggles in school, the more they are being shortchanged in the form of not learning how to overcome these struggles. Several students referenced not having to do homework in high school. Only two students shared that homework was not assigned, but several students, including

Ian, shared that they were able to get by without completing homework or assigned reading and still get decent grades.

"The thing that surprised me most was how much homework I had to do outside of class, especially reading. I usually learn fast, so in high school, I was used to school being pretty easy." At the end of his fall semester in college, Ian received an academic probation letter.

> When I opened it, I panicked because, at first, I thought it meant that I had to drop out. My advisor talked to me about not missing classes and said that if I brought up my GPA spring semester, I would be able to register for fall. I went to every class and did bring it up, but my GPA was still pretty low.

It wasn't until Ian's sophomore year that he made enough significant changes to get on track.

> I figured out that I had to go to class and do the homework and reading and study. In the spring of my sophomore year and in the spring of my junior year I was on the President's Honor Roll, which felt good — especially my junior year because I had really tough classes that semester and an overload from having to retake one of my freshman classes.

Some students know they are failing to learn as they should; they have likely known they are failing for quite some time. Unfortunately, many of these students have not been taught to adapt and adjust, to persist, to do whatever is necessary to succeed, and they have accepted failure in school as an identity. These students likely do not attend college — or they very quickly drop out if they do.

Students like these possibly assume that their classmates are smarter than they are, that others do not struggle with school. Although it may be true that some students shine brighter than others in some areas, we know that the most significant barrier for most struggling students without significant learning disabilities is not intellectual capacity; it is knowing what to do when they hit the wall.

Others (a high percentage of our students — even honor roll students) do not know when they fail. They are often allowed to proceed without correction or adjustment because they finish the work and do a decent job studying for what is on their tests. They are given very little feedback. This appears to work for these students until they attend a university, where minor failures are almost certain and major failures are more than possible in the form of academic expectations they were not prepared to meet.

These students find themselves quickly developing a growth mindset, a set of habits they did not learn before attending college. These students, our majority, often struggle in college; many either drop out or change their course of study to something causing less conflict, less stress, and fewer failures.

The rarest of the students, the most successful by far, attend colleges and universities while being accustomed to correcting their failures. These students are, subsequently, unafraid of failing in the future. They have learned that discomfort is necessary, a requirement, for significant achievement. These students thrive in the college setting—not because they are smarter, but because they have learned to embrace the process when things are not easy. Failure is either already here or coming quickly for our students, all our students. High-impact educators teach them how to react when it does. How?

Comfort Zone versus Growth Zone

High-impact educators know the following and have insisted on making them consistent realities in their classrooms, labs, and auditoriums:

1. Students Must Be Taught How to Push through Discomfort until They Become Successful, and Then It Starts Over with New Challenges

This could be a philosophy for teaching. The high-impact educator knows that it is not likely worth studying or doing if it is in no way challenging. Pointless worksheets or busy work? Three day-long videos with a fluffy assignment to cap it off? Three weeks of a group project, and the teacher never checks in with the groups?

No one interviewed for this book described the most impactful educators as those who kept everything and everyone comfortable. The high-impact educator was described as the relentless governor of learning, someone who routinely pushed students into uncharted territories and somehow always found a way to lead them back smarter than they were before the misery.

Is the high-impact educator sensitive to the collective angst displayed by students who bemoan the extent of effort and skill required? Not really. He knows they can do it. He knows what to do to get them through it. He knows, furthermore, that the real negligence would be to keep them comfortable for so long that future discomforts paralyze them.

2. Successful Students Learn to Expect Discomfort and Have the Essential Habits Required to Turn It into Growth

As those interviewed for this book spoke about their most impactful teachers, a rather humorous theme emerged. The most impactful teachers are not necessarily adored at first. They are often just as much perceived as a discomfort to the students as is the challenging coursework.

Then something happens with these remarkable teachers and their students. Students eventually rise to the ostensibly unreasonable expectations of their teachers to learn that they had it in them to do so all along. No matter how much the researchers asked about the pedagogical strategies that were helpful during the discomfort that got them to the growth zone, it is the high-impact educators that students credit. Long after the discomfort and well into the next set of challenges that are sure to come their way, students recall the educator's steadfast belief in their ability to achieve. Eventually, the students begin to feel more comfortable being uncomfortable.

This is who and what they reference when given the opportunity to speak about the educators who had the most impact on their lives. They talk about the men or women who pushed them to do more than they thought they could do. They talk about the things those teachers said to them when they struggled. They remember the exact words. They talk about how proud they felt to do something they were absolutely certain they could never do. Some cried when they spoke about their most impactful teacher. Those are the teachers who nurtured their sense of purpose and helped them believe in themselves. This is what high-impact educators do.

3. Moving Students Out of Their Comfort Zone Is Necessary for Student Growth and Begins with a Trusting Relationship

Impressive adults are those who have proven capable of turning discomfort into growth. This is not to suggest that any and all discomfort will suffice, we know. High-impact educators are purposeful in their approach and understand that students need different supports and feedback to learn optimally. It is in knowing their students that they are able to tap into their strengths and interests and help them discover their passions. Their students reach the growth zone and beyond when high-impact educators teach them:

- how to study difficult material when giving up is easier;
- how to study longer when more commitment is what is required for success;
- how to read/do homework when it is not fun;
- how to break down challenging tasks into manageable chunks;
- when to put away distracting technology to focus on work;
- how to request feedback;
- how to use feedback;
- how and when to initiate communication with instructors and other sources of support;
- how and when to sacrifice short-term comforts for long-term gains;
- how to use failure as motivation;
- how to tap into strengths to overcome weaknesses;
- how to use successful processes/mindsets that transfer to success in other areas;
- how to develop the self-control needed for new procedures to become habit;

- how to connect new learning to current knowledge and interests; and
- how to develop a sense of purpose.

CLOSING PERSPECTIVE

You cannot swim for new horizons until you have courage to lose sight of the shore. —William Faulkner

The influence of growth mindset and determination has been studied by numerous researchers who have documented its capacity to positively impact success. The work of Dr. Angela Duckworth, a psychology professor at the University of Pennsylvania, is at the forefront of research on grit and growth mindset. Before going into higher education, Duckworth was a secondary math teacher. During her time as a math teacher, she began to observe the effect of effort and grit.

Duckworth was surprised to find that the students who did exceptionally well in her classes were not always the most talented students for whom math came easily. Many of her highest-achieving students were those who worked hard and had the determination to keep trying until they mastered the concepts. Later in her career as a professor, Duckworth and colleagues[1] went on to study what drives achievement by conducting interviews with professionals in investment banking, painting, journalism, academia, medicine, and law.

When professionals were asked what quality distinguishes top performers within their respective fields, they cited grit or a close synonym as often as they cited talent. Similar to Duckworth's experience as a middle and high school math teacher, many professionals observed that the highest achieving in their fields were not necessarily the most talented, but they had extraordinary commitment and determination.

Duckworth and colleagues[2] also studied the practices and traits of thousands of high achieving individuals—undergraduate students attending ivy league colleges, West Point cadets, and young students ranking in the national spelling bee. They found that a major commonality these high-achieving individuals shared was extensive time spent on deliberate practice—not fun practice, not easy practice, not unfocused practice, but effortful and purposeful practice. Duckworth and colleagues reported that of all of the personality traits that predicted how much deliberate practice a person would complete, grit was the top predictor.

Certainly, talent plays a role in success, but those participating in the research for this book revealed that passion and determination often trump talent. High-impact educators know this and convey their belief in each student's ability to achieve at high levels. They, along with parents, help students develop a growth mindset and understanding that significant achievements are accomplished through small incremental steps that are often stalled by setbacks and failures.

High-impact educators, parents, coaches, clergy, and other trusted adults play a pivotal role in helping young people develop a sense of purpose. It is their sense of purpose and belief in themselves that gives them the strength to refrain from retreating to the comfort zone when their work is difficult, harrowing, or monotonous. As students increase their skills and find a sense of purpose, they feed their passion and fuel their grit. Determination is the ultimate intangible.

NOTES

1. A. L. Duckworth, C. Peterson, M. D. Matthews, and D. R. Kelly, "Grit: Perseverance and Passion for Long-Term Goals," *Journal of Personality and Social Psychology* 92, no. 6 (2007): 1087–1101.
2. Ibid.

NINE

Character

GOOD PEOPLE

Miguel was a skinny, good-looking, unfocused, confused, immature, foul-mouthed, frustrated, and frustrating teenager when he attended middle and high school. He was failing most of his courses, his outbursts were nearly daily, and he was a frequent visitor in the dean's office. He was a mess, and he was truly irresistible for his caring teachers and administrators.

His family life was nothing short of barbaric; he had two older brothers infamous for making money on the street (and, as it turned out, in school). His father had been imprisoned multiple times, and his mother lacked the capacity to rise above her situation. Miguel grew up with violent, often-repugnant language, and physical violence was as much of a reality as were daily angst and disappointment. He, his brothers, and his father were all on probation.

Except for the reliability of school lunch, he ate sparsely, typically after his brothers finished eating. He slept when they slept, not before. He wore the same clothes nearly every day. He was taught that women should be objectified, and he only dared talk to his mother when the other males were either gone or passed out. He presented himself as a tough guy who was afraid of nothing. In reality, he spent most of his time in and out of school afraid of almost everything.

What Miguel lived on a daily basis would cripple most people. This was his life, and he had learned enough to know that no trouble from the dean of students could match the stress he endured outside of school. Moreover, he learned that being removed from a class and sent to the office now and then scored him points with his older brothers.

He also learned that coming to the school office to talk to the dean was actually not that bad. The dean of students and Miguel agreed to schedule these discussions with the understanding that Miguel would not intentionally cause trouble to be removed from class (this provision was often broken) and that he was also allowed to tell his brothers he was sent to the office for being disrespectful. The irony of a troubled youth like Miguel forging his way in to discuss life with a person of authority under a simple plea agreement of being allowed to maintain his unruly image is nothing short of Shakespearean. Miguel was hanging on to life by whatever means possible and available. This was a tragedy.

School? Academic progress? College or career readiness? Get real. Miguel was surviving. He would show promising stretches in some of his classes, occasionally turning in assignments. He would participate in physical education, provided the activity did not put him at risk for looking weak or vulnerable. If he made it a few days without becoming a blaring distraction in one of his classes, it was a success.

Miguel's talent was drawing. According to his art teacher, he had a fantastic eye and an uncanny ability to create with his hands. His attendance in art class was spotty at best, however, and assignments were sometimes late, sometimes missed, and often darkly sensationalized.

Imagine completing a take-home art project in Miguel's world. Unthinkable. If Miguel was rested and nourished enough to think, happy enough to function, and had sufficient time to complete art projects in class (provided he was in class), his work was fantastic. Miguel and the dean agreed that his art projects could be stored/hidden in the dean's office so that he could work on things when possible. In reality, Miguel brought only finished pieces to the dean's office. He simply did not want anyone belittling or destroying the most significant work he had ever done in school and likely beyond.

Miguel struggled mightily in school. Why? Was it the reading strategies his teachers implemented in his elementary years coming back to haunt him? Was it faulty, misaligned rubrics serving to confuse Miguel as he attempted to finish his project-based learning component while seeking a solid B in History? Was he not benefitting from one-to-one technology, which would have provided him with a more immediate connection to the world and student achievement?

No. Miguel struggled mightily in school because his life was one catastrophic debacle after another. Shy of either a sizable miracle or years of great adults reframing his life so that success and genuine long-term happiness were at least a possibility, Miguel had no chance in school. Furthermore, when a kid like Miguel (trained in nothing, gifted with no resources, and with very few successful adult role models) fails in school, he almost certainly struggles in life thereafter. This is truth, and it haunts great educators every day.

Did Miguel need reading strategies, clear rubrics, experience with project-based learning, and adequate, purposeful educational technologies? Of course, his reading abilities were nowhere near his grade level, he was a terrible classroom teammate, and his technological acumen was trailing most students ten years younger. But these twenty-first-century staples are nothing—truly nothing—without what must come beforehand: character.

Even if he had learned how to complete and submit his homework in the correct place in the learning management system, Miguel's one-to-one device would not have taught him to use it when and how he should. Reading at grade level or beyond would not have saved him from himself while he remained incapable of showing up for school on time and every day. His school's collaborative learning spaces had no chance of benefitting him as he used these to catch up on his sleep instead of working. His teachers' encouragement could not muster the determination to defy the ingrained expectations of so many others, including himself.

Moreover, academic necessities like reading, critical thinking, and productive technology skills are the result, the glorious side effects of a properly developed character and learned successful habits. The kids armed with the benefits of caring adults who worked to teach them how to be a good person and how to be successful usually cannot help but thrive in school. Academic prowess, in most cases, is a byproduct of great adult influence. The adults in Miguel's life? His father once told him, "If you don't get caught, it ain't against the law."

Character and habits are taught and learned, not inherited. The adults in Miguel's private life failed him because they did not teach him how to be good, productive, and successful for a lifetime. Because of this, the adults in Miguel's school life often felt as though they stood no chance whatsoever in pushing Miguel academically. Instead, they felt helpless, dealing with his unruly, disrespectful display of behavior. They wrestled with limited time to overcome what it would have taken to truly teach him to be college, career, or life ready.

Thriving as a child within school and extracurricular activities? Attending a college or university? Developing as a student in higher education, leading toward either a degree or a promising career path? These require the presence and intentions of adults with great character.

Without beating almost insurmountable odds, kids like Miguel do not attend college. Voices like his were not heard during the interview process for this study. Nonetheless, the authors of this book know that there are issues connected to education and student growth, which extend beyond realities associated with college freshmen, college seniors, and recent college graduates.

Those interviewed for this book shared details about remarkable people in their lives, people who played a hand in changing their life paths for the better.

- "I am not sure I would have gone to college if it weren't for
  _____."
- "I know I would not be where I am today without _____."
- "Mrs. Nelson is the reason I am becoming a math teacher."
- "In our house, college was not about 'if' but about 'where.'"

It takes good people to make good people. Miguel deserved better.

WHAT PARTICIPANTS SHARED

Character is the silent partner in education. It is the assumption so obvious that it often goes unreferenced. No parents of elementary students hope to hand over their children to Miss Trunchbull (*Matilda*), a berating, harsh, and cruel monster. No high school student, aside from Ferris Bueller, is equipped to navigate the wrath of Edward R. Rooney as principal. And although Professor Snape turned out to be a good guy by the end of the *Harry Potter* series, his demeanor in a twenty-first-century university classroom full of freshmen would have him job hunting before Halloween in his first year.

Without question, those interviewed for this book assume that high-character educators are a requirement for both K–12 and college settings. Graduates infinitely credited them as critical to their own character development. No college students or recent college graduates labeled "character" when describing their most impactful teachers. It was, rather, something as obvious as the necessity of having food, water, and oxygen.

Literally hundreds of high-impact educators were described during the interview process for this study—elementary teachers, middle school teachers, high school teachers, professors. These great teachers taught anything and everything—physical education, English, psychology, history, homeroom, and so on. If a teacher was impactful, he or she was impressively remembered and respectfully referenced. What exactly was said about these teachers, aside from the fact that they made a lifelong impact on these young people? How did "character" make this book if the word itself was seldom spoken?

For starters, there is something fascinating in what was never said about the most impactful teachers. No one referenced sarcasm, vulgarity, or cynicism as tools leading toward inspiration. This is not to suggest that these students and recent graduates had no experience with teachers who used these unsavory tactics, however.

The interviewed participants could not resist describing teachers who fell short of being positively impactful for the long-term. Sarcastic, vulgar, cynical teachers and coaches exist, the participants assured, and their positive impact on college-bound students is either nonexistent or short-lived. "Most of my college professors have their Ph.D., and they know their content, but not all of them are necessarily good at teaching—they don't all know how to convey it."

> My statistics professor would get super annoyed when we didn't understand what he was talking about. One time when I told him after class it wasn't making sense to me, he said, 'Look, I can't explain it any better than I already have. Not everyone is cut out for this level.' Then he told me to watch an online video and just walked away. I was trying my best to learn it, but he just made me feel stupid.

Harsh language, sour behavior, or indifference from a teacher or a coach do not translate well into effective, lifelong habits for students. These instructors may mean well; they may use their sarcasm to reach students on their level—a veritable shock and awe effort aimed at snapping students into the desired, realistic present. "Wow, Mr. Ventre swore. . . . He must be serious. . . . I had best pay attention."

Except, it does not work. When these kids become college students (particularly college seniors), they roll their eyes while describing teachers who needed crass directives and cynicism to inspire. The interviewed participants have all been exposed to higher education and, in most cases, a higher level of thinking and communication (chapter 7).

Perhaps sarcasm got their attention when they were in middle school and used it themselves to make sense and describe nearly everything in their world. Even then, it did not inspire. Sarcasm, vulgarity, and cynicism can be humorous at times; it can have a cutting edge so appealing for young people. Inspiration, however, comes from places much more contemplative, according to those interviewed.

When asked to describe their most impactful teachers, the college students and recent college graduates typically appeared to dive deep into memories reserved for cherished, incredibly rare people. The following traits became themes for the character of those described as high-impact educators:

- Kind:

> I will always remember my seventh- and eighth-grade science teacher. She was extremely kind and personable. She taught me that it's okay to be yourself. She was quirky, and kind of a nerd like me. . . . She'd get super excited about science, and everyone liked her.

- Approachable:

> My high school junior and senior English teacher was a genuine human. I wasn't the best English student, and she cared to make sure I learned. You could ask her any question, and she'd say, "It's good that you asked," and she'd explain things and made sure I understood.

- Empathetic:

I think the best teachers have empathy. They are willing to explain what they are doing multiple times. The worst say it and don't go back. . . . It's not even on their radar that students aren't getting it. Mr. Rabar was my favorite math teacher. If I didn't do well on a test, he'd take the time to make sure I understood it, even if it was after the test. He'd say, "What's important is that you get it because you are going to use this moving forward and he'd allow me to earn some points back." I went back and visited him on fall break. Learning is a lot more than a GPA.

- Strong-willed:

Dr. Griesowsky is fearless. She's not afraid to tell you what she thinks, and she'll do what it takes to help you get better. I had a fear of public speaking, and she made it clear that I would be required to participate in every presentation. On the day of my first presentation, I told her that I didn't feel well, and I seriously thought I was going to be sick. She told me that I'd feel better in approximately four minutes (which is how long my presentation was supposed to be), and she motioned me to go to the front while she announced that we were getting started. The entire time I was presenting, she was nodding in assurance at the back of the room. I had no idea if I was even making sense, but I figured if she was nodding and smiling, I would keep going.

- Smart:

My History teacher knows everything about history, and he can explain it in a way that is interesting and relevant. One of the things I like about him is that he's always pointing out how to integrate information into our other classes and why it's important in life. He'll flat out ask us, "Why does this matter?" He makes me think about how events in 1791 apply to today.

- Consistent:

I owe a lot to Mrs. Nelson. Not everyone liked her because they thought she was too hard. She pushed me and consistently had us write. We wrote something every day, and we wrote a lot of papers. She'd give me honest feedback, and she would have regular writing conferences with us. She'd remind us all of the time that even for professional writers, easy reading is hard writing. She helped me feel proud of my writing.

Educators with these qualities may or may not be the most popular teachers in the moment. Many of those interviewed admitted that the character lessons being modeled and taught from their most impactful teachers took some time (years, in some examples) to be understood and appreciated. Learning decency and humility takes time, it seems—time to realize that impressive character is not something one displays when he or she is being watched, something that appears only when things are going well, or something that happens because it is part of a school district or university expectation.

Great character, rather, is a personality trait of high-impact educators. They know who they need to be for their students, not merely for today, but for their futures. The participants in this study raved about high-impact educators for one remarkable reason: they improved the lives of their students. They took the time to teach them the value of being mindful, kind, and empathetic, even—and especially—when they were acting otherwise. High-impact educators see the best in students and helped them get past their worst. "He told me I was better than how I was acting. . . . If it wasn't for Mr. Taylor, I wouldn't be who I am."

We know that learning measurable curriculum is important (more important than most recognize). We know that developing lifelong habits like critical thinking (chapter 3), creativity (chapter 4), collaboration (chapter 5), autonomy (chapter 6), communication (chapter 7), and determination (chapter 8) are vital for a life of success. But without character, none of it seems to matter.

Character is the compass within us. The interviewed participants were often visibly emotional when describing those who selflessly dedicated themselves to making the student a better version of herself. Reading, writing, math, history, art, band, choir, basketball, hockey, theater, student council—these are important, we adults know. There is good to be found within all of these—and some are absolutely essential.

Yet, we do not necessarily learn calculus just because it is good for us. The interviewed participants shared that in the absence of a mature adult's mindset related to learning difficult academic content, they committed themselves to learning difficult content because they could not justify disappointing the kind, empathetic, strong-willed, brilliant, and consistently good human being teaching this content. "If this is important enough for Ms. Honey, it is important enough for me."

Elementary, middle, and high school students are usually not yet mature enough to recognize this. Even college freshmen are typically too young and unlearned in the world's subtleties to fully understand. College seniors and recent college graduates, however, see it. The most impactful people in their lives? The people who taught them the most? The people who taught and modeled that accomplishment is best used with respect, decency, and humility? The best people.

WHAT IT MEANS FOR US

It is easy to believe that good people, those respectful, decent men and women who carry themselves with an aura of humility, are simply born to be that way. We see these people as adults, and it can be difficult to imagine they were ever (or could have been) knuckleheads. Likewise, it is convenient to feel that disrespectful, wrong-doing selfish people result from something as primitive as genetics.

We may be tempted to believe that the collection of all of us, those who do great things in the world, those who perform unthinkable acts of evil, and those who find themselves in the middle, is the accumulating result of nothing more than chance. Those great students in third-period A.P. English, those kids who were destined for college the day they were born? Good luck.

That crew struggling to pass fifth-period U.S. History, some of whom have been in trouble with the law, all of whom are nowhere close to reading at grade level? Bad luck. The auditorium full of college freshmen who, despite knowing the semester has obviously begun, have not yet considered where or how to purchase the class text for Biology 101? Recurring nightmare bad luck.

Nonsense. Aside from issues outside of anyone's influence (severe mental illness, for example), people become who they were raised and educated to become. Our students? They are a reflection of their parents' and teachers' abilities and expectations. Like anyone reading this book, the interviewed participants have made decisions about who they want to be and how they want to conduct their daily affairs.

They are, admittedly, free agents for their decisions and character. Yet, when asked to reflect upon how they got to their current spot in life or who helped them get there, not one interviewee responded with a tone of isolation. They credited others for their good fortune, even if there was strong support for impressive autonomy.

The luck, if it existed for these participants, was found in the fact that impressive role-models were available for them when they were learning how to be adults—and that these people cared enough to both possess and teach them respect, decency, and humility.

Behavior—good, bad, and otherwise—is learned. It would be wonderful if every K–12 or university student we educate were gifted with a morally sound, virtuous mother and father at home. Our job as educators would be much easier if respect, decency, and humility came prepackaged.

Education would be reimagined and redefined if all students were raised at home to understand the connection between their attitudes, behaviors, decisions, kindness, and the effect on being successful in life. It would be much easier to teach students if all parents were like the best of parents. It is also true, however, that our students would be much more likely to thrive as scholars and professionals while being better human beings if all teachers were like the best teachers.

We cannot hide from this responsibility; we cannot be high-impact educators while simultaneously holding that "this kid would be successful if he weren't such a jerk." Are some students jerks? Yes, absolutely. High-impact educators know a significant number of strong, impressive, decent adults were jerks as children and adolescents. The reason they have transitioned from intolerable to impressive and strong with character? The strong, impressive, decent adults in their lives did not quit on the student.

High-impact educators are called to be the strong, impressive, decent adults. Their curriculum is challenging, and their teaching strategies are effective beyond recognition—but they accomplish so much more than delivering measurable academics. High-impact educators—according to over 150 college freshmen, college seniors, and recent college graduates spread over eleven states—teach and embody respect, decency, and humility. These values can and should be emphasized at every turn within our auditoriums, classrooms, labs, hallways, lunchrooms, and gymnasiums.

CLOSING PERSPECTIVE

No participants in this study referenced school policies or philosophies. They credited great adults, those respectful, decent, humble educators who cared about them enough to make certain they learned both curriculum and character. Academic growth and character development are connected, furthermore. The more respectful, decent, and humble one becomes, the more he or she is open to growth. High-impact educators know that developing either curriculum attainment or personal character without the other growing alongside is either futile or dangerous.

Miguel, for example, was not learning about comma usage and essay strategies for the ACT when he visited the dean's office. He was learning that it is selfish to make the world (his classmate and his teachers) pay for his bad day, that being respected is not the same as being feared, that respect only comes to someone when it is also given.

The dean and Miguel often spoke about women. The world is full of strong women capable of being lovely and kind while also thinking for themselves as equals, the dean would remind Miguel. Consequently, when Miguel's female teachers pushed him to be more than he was, they were not acting as condescending "witches"; they were actually complimenting him by recognizing his potential.

Miguel would get a lesson a week, it seemed, on how he communicated with his teachers. Vulgarity works to add shock value and works for stupid people, but his teachers were too experienced to be shocked by him and not the least bit dull. We cannot be taken seriously, Miguel was frequently reminded, if we mumble and avoid eye contact when trying to speak to someone. Successful people, Miguel would hear time and time again, do not sabotage themselves when they speak; they know whom they are talking to, and they know how their words will be received.

There was no magic tonic in school for Miguel to make up for the disadvantages he suffered, but that did not excuse the educators in his life from working with him to be more and better than he was displaying. Miguel did not know how to be a decent, contributing member of the society we call school. The dean and Miguel's teachers tirelessly worked with him so he could learn as many truths as possible and hopefully find a way to apply these lessons to life outside of school.

High-impact educators do this for an endless line of reasons, not the least being the realization that the biggest difference between the most successful of high school graduates and Miguel is not the GPA, the scholarship opportunities, or the plans after high school. Rather, it is the fact that our most successful students know how to successfully handle themselves in a complicated world, and Miguel did not. Character? We can call this whatever we want. Academic growth is both impossible and insignificant without it.

Whether it is a safe growth zone for college-bound students like those interviewed for this book or possibly the last hope for students like Miguel, a school's culture and climate, the authors have learned, are only as powerful as its teachers. Superb schools benefit from high-impact educators who define *culture* and *climate* with kindness, empathy, strength, intelligence, work ethic, and consistency.

Emphasizing anything too far removed from these traits of great character is pointless. Schools and universities are called to more than dole out diplomas. High-impact educators are remembered for seeing the potential good in every student. They take the time to teach intellectual habits and character habits essential to developing the whole person.

Mission statements and educational philosophies at all levels should reflect a commitment to character development. Still, it will take more than policy and curriculum to prepare struggling students for post-secondary educational opportunities or help kids like Miguel, a young man dangerously close to losing all hope for a productive life, find a way out of perpetuating struggle. Only amazing adults do this.

III

Relationships and Student Growth

TEN

Emphasizing Relationships

THE RECIPROCITY OF LEARNING AND RELATIONSHIPS

Relationships matter. People need human contact; sometimes, we crave it. We want to be known, understood, and liked—and most of us desire to truly know and understand others. We benefit from quality relationships in a multitude of ways. They keep us physically and emotionally healthier; they provide a necessary home base for our safety and training us how to harmoniously coexist with others whether we are thriving or merely surviving. Our relationships, in fact, play the lead role in teaching us about ourselves.

For these reasons and countless others, relationships often become the defining moments of education. Anyone struggling to reconcile with this reality need only listen to any group of two or more adults recollect their school years. When we speak about our elementary years, what do we share? Has any forty-five-year-old ever reminisced about learning the multiplication tables? "Wasn't it glorious transitioning from adding and subtracting to multiplication and division?"

No, we remember our best friends from elementary school. We recall the events of recess as though our life depends on it. We learned the essentials, of course, but that happened concurrently with learning about and contributing to the human stories of others, while simultaneously figuring out how we fit into the world.

How about our first school dance? Our first crush? The group science project that we were certain would change the world? The middle school years are vital for academic growth; if students can reach grade-level proficiency or above in these years and relate well with others, research shows, the odds are in their favor that they will be ready for the next level and beyond. Yet it is the relationships that define these years in our

99

minds. We remember eating lunch with friends, participating in great class discussions, and we remember our favorite teachers and how they made us feel.

Indeed, high-impact educators know the significance of the middle years when literature and math become more complex and abstract when proving competency in these areas is paramount. High-impact educators also know that if a student's relationships are not developing appropriately at this time, their academic growth is often impacted.

And so it goes with high school. Relationships continue to play a significant role in student growth throughout the high school years as adolescents more clearly envision the person they want to become and learn from others how to navigate the world more effectively. One need only consider the nationwide, yearly gatherings in the form of high school reunions. Old friends come together to reminisce, laugh, and share their new realities with old friends. We do not meet every five to ten years to celebrate the ACT.

It could be argued that a child's education happens alongside and often through the building of relationships with peers and adults alike. Curriculum attainment is necessary, for certain. Our students are headed toward adult struggles without competence in reading, communication, and math. Whether students fully comprehend this reality or not, this is not what gets most of them out of bed and to school on time every day. Without the magic elixir of relationships (in the form of clubs, sports, music, activities, or simply a proximity to friends and caring adults), learning will suffer.

For high-impact educators, however, the relationships created are not at all a mysterious accident. They are intentional. They are a necessity. High-impact educators know that students learn more and better when they experience healthy, productive relationships in school. Those interviewed for this book agree.

WHAT PARTICIPANTS SHARED

I want my teachers to know me as a person. —Lucas, freshman

Students Want to Be Known

When asked what she wished her current or future teachers knew about her, one freshman answered,

> I want my professors to know that I'm a hard worker, and I hope that they know me enough to know that I don't slack and that I will get things done. If I ask them for help or tell them that I don't understand, it's because I care about the class. I'm not giving up, and I don't want them to just give up on me and think I can't make it through the

program. I like learning, and I like the atmosphere of challenging learning.

Many college students talked about being in classes where they rarely, if ever, spoke to some of their professors.

> One of my professors doesn't know anything about me. . . . He doesn't even know my name. We only have a month left of the semester, and just this week, he said, "What's your name?" and then found my name on his sheet without looking at me and started writing as he was grading our presentation.

> I haven't missed a class or a single deadline, but he has no idea who I am. When I got my grade, there wasn't any helpful written down; it just said, "solid presentation, 45/50." That's B or maybe a B+, but I have no idea what I can do better or what I did that was good. He never interacts with me or any of the students.

Bethany, a college senior double majoring in political science and philosophy, spoke with nostalgic fondness about her elementary and high school teachers. Mrs. Halverson, her eleventh-grade American history teacher, in particular, who she often talked to before and after class, had a lasting impact on her learning by teaching her the difference between information and knowledge. Information is readily available, she discovered, but knowledge requires a journey of critical study. "Mrs. Halverson taught me to enjoy the journey toward knowledge, and that changed everything for me—especially in college."

Students interviewed for this book often spoke about the subject and the teacher inseparably. If they have a positive relationship with the teacher, they tend to have a positive attitude toward the subject and are willing to dedicate themselves to the learning. An affable college freshman named Lucas was genuinely invested in the relational aspect of learning, and it was quickly apparent that he was someone who would be difficult not to like.

> I want my teachers to know me as a person. If the course is one that I don't like or one that I'm just not as good at, but I like the teacher, and they know me, I always end up liking the class. If I know the teacher, I can ask questions and talk to them . . . even about things not directly related to the class. When there's a good relationship, I'm more invested, and I'll work hard until I get it.

When asked what their most impactful teachers do or have done differently, nearly all the participants in this study specified these teachers' insistence on knowing the students as individuals. Whether this was reflected by asking students about their extra-curricular activities, remembering the names of their older siblings, enthusiastically greeting them both in and out of the classroom, or simply asking students questions and maintaining a respectful presence long enough to hear a response, the most impactful teachers demonstrate an unwavering commitment to know the students they teach.

This is how students know their teachers care. There is important academic content to learn throughout the K–12 and college experience, participants know, but some of it was either an incredible struggle or almost completely neglected altogether for these participants. So often, the difference between learning difficult, significant content, and failing to grow can be condensed into the quality of the relationship the student has with the educator. If the student feels like she is known, she feels like she has a powerful ally who will not disappear when learning becomes difficult. According to those interviewed, being known gives them the strength and courage to work through discomfort.

Feeling anonymous, however, can have a crippling effect on a student as he is pushing to learn difficult content. A student may be hesitant to ask for assistance, clarification, or other feedback if he feels as though his instructor does not know him. The participants for this study were clear on this issue: if the teacher does not know the student, the student is far less likely to reach out for assistance. This is only natural, for our students prefer to be known for their positive attributes before they are expected to expose themselves for their shortcomings.

Students Recognize and Value Empathetic Teachers

Throughout their development, the challenges students navigate, whether academic, social, or emotional, are more manageable when the people at the center of that navigation show empathy. This finding, perhaps more than any other, highlighted the importance of humanizing our work in education.

One college senior who interviewed in the research of this book illustrated the long-term impact of empathy in teaching and learning. Katelyn was a high school valedictorian who scored slightly above average on the ACT with a below-average score on the math section. At the time of her interview, she was heading into the last semester of her nursing major with a 4.0 career total GPA.

> I think the most important qualities in a teacher are to be nice and personable, to be able to teach the content well and also to be forgiving and empathetic. In high school and middle school, math has been a low point. My brain doesn't function well in that subject. I had to get over the low points in math and not get down about school. The repetitive failure made it hard to find motivation, but then I had Mr. Effertz for math in my junior year of high school.

It was clear that Mr. Effertz understood that not every student can reach grade-level mastery in a regular fifty-minute class period and he was creative in finding ways to reach them inside and outside of the scheduled period. "He would show me different ways and tell me that I can always try a different pattern. In the morning he would review with students if they came in for tutoring time."

On Fridays, Mr. Effertz invited AP math students to come to his classroom in the morning and join the study groups to give provide help.

> He'd say that he would pay them in tasty lemon loaf. Mr. Effertz always brought lemon loaf on Fridays and said he made for us, and we'd always joke with him and tell him that we knew his wife made it. He'd walk around and check in with our study groups, beaming about how good the lemon loaf was. If we couldn't get something, he'd say, "Don't worry if you don't have it; you just don't have it yet. . . . That's why you're here."

Five years after Mr. Effert's encouragement, support, tutoring time, and Friday lemon loaf, his influence on Katelyn's learning continued.

> He helped me get past my math anxiety, and I finally started to understand it. If it weren't for him, I would have never made it through College Algebra, and it is required for my degree. I've always wanted to be a nurse, and I know it would not be possible without Mr. Effertz.

Tony, a college senior, affirmed the value of compassionate relationships.

> The best teachers have compassion. You don't have to be a genius to be a good teacher. . . . Don't take this personally [he directed this at the two educators interviewing him]. Of course, you have to know your content, but some of the most intelligent teachers I've had have been the worst. They can't communicate it to their students, maybe because they don't develop a relationship with us.

Having a teacher or professor know you is a baseline for success in school, and having that teacher or professor empathize with you is truly the difference between being a school-based acquaintance and being members of the same extraordinary team. "The most impactful teachers," according to one interviewed participant and echoed by countless others, "understand me, but they aren't trying to be my friend."

Empathetic educators are valued by their students years after their time together because they knew their students the right way. As trusted adults, they model what it means to look outward, beyond our personal experiences and perspectives and understand the circumstances of others. Those interviewed for this book explained that their most impactful teachers, regardless of grade level, have not been their buddies.

Instead, they steadfastly embody empathy by being caring adults. Fun? Exciting? Energetic? Funny? Perhaps, even likely, but never at the cost of being a pal when what students truly need is a friendly, empathetic adult who strategically teaches challenging content and invaluable life lessons.

It is worth noting that many of those interviewed admitted that their realizations about appropriately empathetic adult teachers took time. This makes sense, for we are children when some of our most impactful teaches leave their mark. If one's most impactful teacher was a seventh-grade science teacher, an educator who managed to teach content which so often causes struggle while at the same time helping to guide the kid through the stress of middle school and early adolescence, it is unlikely he or she would have maturity enough to comprehend this teacher's greatness in the moment.

There Is a Union between Teacher-Student Relationship Quality and Feedback Quality

One college freshman acknowledged that when she entered college, she found it difficult to accept criticism, until she was criticized for not being able to take criticism:

> Dr. Purcell said, "Listen, you can't scoff every time I tell you that you need to do something different. You have to be able to take feedback and criticism." I didn't even realize that I was scoffing, but I really like Dr. Purcell, and I knew that he was trying to help me, so I started using his criticism to get better.

The everyday seemingly small connections we make with students play a large role in motivating them and making them feel valued.

> The best teachers reach out to you. I worked a lot harder for those teachers who cared about me and appeared to care about my success. One of my favorite teachers taught a night class. . . . He'd ask, "What's something interesting going on today?" He'd build rapport. He was friendly. When he'd give suggestions for improvement, he was always enthusiastic, like he couldn't wait for you to try it and see the improvement. It made me want to try harder for him.

One of the most significant findings of the research conducted for this book centers on the power of teacher feedback. High-impact educators challenge their students to the point of having to make (substantial, at times) corrections and adjustments. They make a habit of removing students from their comfort zones and positioning them in growth zones. This process requires rich, specific feedback—and, as communicated by droves of those interviewed for this book, that feedback will not resonate with the students without first having a strong, productive relationship established.

Students Will Attempt What Causes Them Discomfort if They Have an Exceptional Working Relationship with Their Teacher

Making corrections and adjustments requires that students are willing to collaborate with the teacher (chapter 5), are open to communication even when it is critical (chapter 7), have a growth mindset (chapter 8), and have the humility necessary to acknowledge their current ability/performance level is not yet good enough (chapter 9). These matters are not realized without the trust corresponding with a high-yielding relationship between the student and an adult high-impact educator.

High-Impact Educators Make All Classroom Relationships Better

Something interesting happens when college students and recent college graduates describe their most impactful teachers. The description usually begins with an appreciation of what the educator accomplished with this particular student—a recap of the student-teacher one-on-one success story. Shortly thereafter, the account evolves to an appreciation of the entire educational environment.

Almost all students are educated while in the presence of many other students; it is nearly impossible to learn without participating in relationships. High-impact educators, according to those interviewed, maximize all relationships (teacher-student, student-student, etc.) in an academic setting so that growth is realized for everyone. This is perhaps the most amazing trait a high-impact educator possesses. Interviewed participants raved about their most amazing teachers who somehow:

- knew their content as experts;
- knew each student as an individual; and
- knew their class (however large or small) as a whole.

The high-impact educator knows that there are only so many opportunities available for those Aristotle–Plato, one-on-one moments of teaching. When these opportunities are available, he or she makes them count. Most of the time, however, the educational process is far more convoluted. The high-impact educator is speaking with several students, knowing somehow the right words required to reach both "all of them" and "all of them as individuals." The high-impact educator also successfully positions students amongst themselves, trusting that the relationship skills have been developed within his class to the point that students will grow even when the teacher is not directly leading instruction.

Graduates remember these remarkable teachers and their phenomenal learning environments not merely because the classrooms were fun (although they often were), or because the teacher was pleasant, upbeat, and funny (although she often was), or because they somehow got along with a diverse group of classmates in the school setting (although they probably did). They remember these remarkable teachers and their dynamic and supportive learning environments because all these positive relationships existed while playing a major role in academic growth.

WHAT IT MEANS FOR US

With Some Unique Exceptions, Students Learn Better When They Feel Like Their Teachers Know Them, Like Them, Respect Them, and Believe in Them

The outliers are too few to address. Present at every level of an effective education from elementary through college is the vitality of a thriving collectivity of relationships. The overwhelming majority of students, including every interviewed participant for this book, either benefit from or struggle because of the relationships associated with their education.

We cannot have effective schools without high-impact educators who know, like, respect, and believe in their students. Furthermore, these impactful teachers possess the ability to establish and maintain positive, purposeful relationships with both the entirety of their students and individuals. The "whole class" relationship affects everyone as individuals—and every individual relationship plays a significant role in the whole class.

The learning does not occur simply because the students are known well and respectfully treated. High-impact educators also know their content and how to teach it (chapter 11). However, the high-impact educator knows that if any link in the chain of teacher-student, teacher-students, student-student relationships is damaged, learning will suffer.

Learning Effective Twenty-First-Century Skills and Habits Requires Strong Relationships

This is the little secret every skilled educational leader already knows. Learning does not happen without strong habits. Can a student ace the tests and earn an A while displaying a poor work ethic and coming late four days a week? Unfortunately, yes. But learning? Learning is a different issue altogether.

Students are not learning if they are comfortable being late four out of five days; they are simply showing what they have already learned. Students are not learning if nothing is challenging them; they are doing what is required to advance. Thinking critically, showing creativity, collaborating, using autonomy, communicating effectively, working diligently, and displaying great character will not happen for students if they have not been privy to relationships that both modeled and expected these habits.

High-impact educators use these twenty-first-century skills and habits as the foundation for everything else. Grammar? Sentence structure? Formulating and testing a hypothesis? None of these happen before an impactful teacher uses their incredible relationship skills first to teach winning habits.

High-Impact Educators Build Strong Relationships with All Students, Even Those Resistant to Forming That Bond

Some students are difficult to know well. They may be terribly insecure, they could be shy, or they may struggle with the content. Perhaps they are dealing with some social issues, or their home life is unstable, or they are facing a dilemma they are ill-equipped and ill-prepared to tackle. It could be anything, but this does not stop the high-impact educator from building the relationship and teaching relational skills.

It is sometimes easy maintaining a great relationship with the student council president and the captain of the football team. Some youths are luckier than others, and this makes it easier for them to know and be known. The most impactful teachers, however, are equally drawn to students who resist the relationships they so badly need.

They know that for some students, school is the only place where they will learn critical life skills essential for forming positive relationships and making good decisions. High-impact educators are committed to teaching those skills and know that they have no chance of doing so successfully without first forming trusting relationships with students.

The high-impact educator is an adult, unafraid of "stepping in" because they know that their students need healthy, productive relationships in order to grow. They do not need the student to divulge information about the state of affairs at home; they need the student to trust that, no matter what, this relationship is safe, consistent, and will lead to growth.

High-Impact Educators Are Not Friends

The relationships students need from their most impactful teachers is more important, more caring, and more strategic than a friendship. K–12 and university students need friendships, of course, and these relationships are best formed with their peer groups. The best of friends are "there" when needed; they love, they accept, and they support. High-impact educators are adults. They are friendly, but they more resemble the best of parents than the best of friends.

CLOSING PERSPECTIVE

K–12 and college students need to know we care—and they are willing to accept almost any version of authentic caring we can provide. The high-impact educators described by interviewed participants have a multitude of faces, teaching styles, and personalities. The authors heard a twenty-two-year-old man describe his fourth-grade teacher, a woman who was likely in her fifties when she taught him, as though she had saved him from a life of ruin.

The interviewed participant had no memory of his teacher's affinity for athletics; she likely never spoke about sports. Interestingly, this young man was a prominent high school and college athlete. The teacher he described was not particularly cool, nor was she described as funny. Her personality did not glow in the dark. She cared.

The relationship quality between an impactful teacher and his students will override almost all other details (with the exception of content expertise and teaching ability). That stated, in the end, if students do not grow, improve, or *learn*, our caring was only a fraction of what it could have been for the students.

The best of us—the high-impact educators like the fourth-grade teacher who knew or cared little about sports, was not in the least bit cool, and has likely never been described as funny—create and maintain relationships with every student to teach both challenging curriculum and irreplaceable life skills and habits. These are the teachers remembered by students; they are the teachers responsible for student growth.

ELEVEN
Emphasizing Student Growth

I had not even gathered my data yet, and she was asking me, "What have you learned?" Professor Rowan asked that question all the time. The answer is, a lot. Every day. —Elizabeth, senior

Chapter 10 outlines what public K–12 educational administrators have been emphasizing and prioritizing for years—nothing happens without great relationships. This accurate assessment has led to an overhaul in K–12 plans and procedures. We can no longer justify attempting to disseminate curriculum without knowing our students and proving ourselves to be empathetic both in and out of the classroom setting.

The high-impact educators capable and willing to foster these relationships thrive because their students feel safe to tackle challenging new tasks and are more willing to accept the essential feedback that leads to growth. Educational leaders know that when students have exceptional relationships with their teachers, they are more willing to step outside of their comfort zone to take the healthy risks needed for growth.

Thus, great stress has been given (especially in K–12 education) to improving relationships in schools. The interview process for a K–12 school teacher, for example, is typically layered with questions designed to reveal one's philosophies or dispositions related to collegial unity, teamwork, dealing with "difficult people" (and perhaps revealing if the interviewee is the difficult one) and, most importantly, the capacity to know and empathize with all students.

From there, teacher evaluations follow a similar path. How well are you working with the members of your Professionl Learning Communities? How effective are you with your classroom management? Do peers like you? Do students like you? Relationships matter in school, and teachers have clearly received the message.

However, the emphasis on great relationships in schools has the potential of luring educational leaders into being neglectful of other vitalities. We too often assume that our quest for smiles, laughter, and comfort in the school setting is the endgame itself. Students will learn more effectively if they are in the right environment, we believe. This is almost true. If incredible, life-changing student growth was akin to making a glass of chocolate milk, we too often mistakenly forget to mix in the milk after the glass was given its ample dosage of chocolate.

The college freshmen, college seniors, and recent college graduates spoke at length about their most impactful teachers and the ability of these educators to relate well with students. They did not stop there, however. Their most impactful teachers have also taught them things they likely would not have learned without that relationship. Their best teachers did not stop at knowing them well and being empathetic; they started there.

Educational leaders in today's K–12 districts and universities too often mistakenly assume that high-quality teaching and feedback are occurring in all classrooms. We hire for relationship skills and emphasize them at all stages of teaching, for we know from both personal experience and almost an almost endless supply of research that learning is a struggle without those healthy connections.

The participants for this study warned us against this shortsightedness. Relationships matter, but we do not work behind the desk at the YMCA. High-impact educators are more than a friendly, welcoming presence in a school or on campus; they are impactful because they are facilitating deep learning.

WHAT PARTICIPANTS SHARED

High-Impact Educators "Know Us, Help Us, and Challenge Us"

What are the most impactful teachers using their incredible relationship skills for if not for the realization of student growth? Teachers and professors can know and like and enjoy their students until the end of time, yet these pleasantries become little more than daily social gatherings if the time spent together does not result in growth.

When asked about her most impactful educators, a senior science major needed no time to ponder her options:

> My most impactful teacher was definitely Professor Rowan. I loved her class because we could choose options that we were most interested in, as long as they matched the learning goals. For my research project, I decided to gather data using a survey. I was super excited to conduct the survey because I was interested in proposing healthier choices in

the cafeteria, and I was hopeful that I could document the need and show that other students also supported it.

Elizabeth described scrupulously revising her research question three times with feedback from Professor Rowan before submitting it with her survey:

> She had a way of helping us think, and she made me want to learn, but she was never disparaging, even when she thought we could do better. We did all kinds of hands-on projects in her class, and she would always remind us that the first draft of our product should be our best effort but never our last effort. . . .
>
> When I had my research design consult with Professor Rowan, she said that she liked my revised research question because it was clear, measurable, and interesting. That made me proud because my first version had been rather mediocre.

When Professor Rowan shifted to Elizabeth's survey, she asked her to read some questions aloud. "As I was reading, I started to see that this would not be my last effort. . . . I had work to do."

Professor Rowan's feedback was thorough and specific; however, the learning remained in the lap of the student.

> She asked me, 'Does that sound clear? Have you asked any leading questions? Why does that matter? Did you align to your research question? What data will you need to present to . . . the food service director?" I had not even gathered my data yet, and she was asking me, "What have you learned?" Professor Rowan asked that question all the time. The answer is—*a lot*. Every day.

College seniors and recent college graduates begin to identify and describe their most impactful teachers differently than they perceived them even a few years prior. "We have friends," one college senior shared. "I don't need any more friends. I need to learn what I need to know." This young woman was studying to become a respiratory therapist, and the National Board Exam was on her horizon and moving closer by the day.

Ironically, as students grow beyond high school graduation and transition into a successful college career, many often view their most impactful teachers, past or present, as revered mentors. This is not to suggest that college students across the nation have movie nights with their third-grade teacher and their History 101 professor in tow, it more elucidates the truth that, in the end, students cherish the teachers who most successfully challenged them to know or do more. They remember the teachers who motivated them to invest themselves to get to deeper learning. These are the teachers and professors who are more likely to have incredible relationships with former students.

High-Impact Educators Are Good at Teaching Their Content

How much more obvious can this be? The interviewed participants fleshed it out; however, because "good at teaching their content" has more significance than merely stating, "Professor Rowan is good at teaching Industrial Biotechnology." It is about being good at teaching in a way that leads to students learning and applying the content.

Professor Rowan used problem-based learning, inquiry, feedback, and self-evaluation, and she encouraged students to learn from their mistakes, reject mediocrity, and pursue their passions. Her approach was not dominated by lecture, but she most definitely knew her content. It guided her curriculum design, observations, questions, feedback, assessment, and recognition that students could go deeper and do better. College students and recent college graduates offered a resounding and unified declaration that high-impact educators are good at teaching their content because:

- "They really know their content,"
- "They challenge me."
- "They give good feedback."
- "They explain it in different ways."

And:

- "They really know how to teach it."
- "They are organized and clear."
- "They help me understand it."
- "They inspire me to work hard."

It is not enough to love kids and build fantastic relationships. The most impactful teachers use their love of kids to drive academics into the quality worlds of their students. No one enjoys learning English grammar, for it is a seemingly endless line of rules associated with one of the most snooty and contradicting languages on Earth: English. Too bad. It needs to be learned, so they teach it.

Do they make it fun? No, English grammar is not fun. The high-impact English teacher, however, may be loads of fun. He may be a whirling dervish of pleasantries, quick wit, astounding insight, and communication and relationship skills enough to lead a cult following. It is because of these, perhaps, that his students will trust his insistence that they improve their grammar, but "fun" will have nothing to do with it. This extraordinary teacher, more than anything else, (a) really knows his grammar; (b) is transparent about why grammar matters; and (c) really knows how to make certain his students learn grammar.

High-Impact Educators Provide Constructive Criticism via Great (and Frequent) Feedback

This is a crucial caveat to teaching challenging curriculum to students. Specifically, it means the material likely will be addressed in a multitude of forms and fashions, and it will be finessed to meet the needs of the class as a whole (however large or small) and those of individual students. Challenging content is not often learned at first sight or sound—if it were, we are wise to reevaluate how we define *challenging*. Instead, substantial learning in the growth zone requires trial and error—then more and more trials until the concept is learned and applied.

According to those interviewed for this study, the most impactful teachers are not necessarily those who give the greatest lectures or devise the most inclusive environment for small group discussions. These are fantastic attributes for a teacher or professor, but high-impact educators are described and defined as those who painstakingly, constructively criticize their students' development and progress.

It is not simply that the most impactful teachers use feedback with their teaching; it is that the rich and frequent feedback is itself the teaching. The amazing lecture? The fun and engaging group discussions? The well-thought-out lesson plan resulting in a perfect one-page written reflection? Of course. But the high-impact educator knows the difference between students harmoniously playing along with the daily lesson plan versus actually learning that lesson's objectives.

The interviewees, moreover, did not isolate a certain "style" of teacher or professor they define as most impactful. There was no belittling of the oft-chastised "sage on the stage," nor was there an avalanche of praise for the educators who, in accordance with contemporary twenty-first-century educational ideologies, ensured the classroom environment was learner-centered. These were merely minor details for participants. The most impactful teachers have teaching methods as unique as their varied personalities, yet they all share this: it is not effective teaching if the students are not learning, and if learning of knowledge and skills is absent, so too is student growth.

Feedback. The college students and recent college graduates saved their highest praise for teachers who refused to allow them to "get by." Quality feedback requires content expertise as well as relationship and communication skills in the form of collaboration. Mostly, it requires an insistence that students learn and grow. In the end, this is what students take from their teachers.

High-Impact Educators Reward Curiosity

When students were allowed a pathway to learning that allowed choice to connect to their interests and passions, they were motivated to step outside their comfort zone to be challenged in new ways. Students frequently spoke about the contagious nature of their teachers' curiosity and passion, as well as the increased depth of learning they could achieve when allowed to explore their own curiosities. Whether building curiosity or leveraging it, high-impact educators understand the role that curiosity plays in learning and growth.

High-Impact Educators Believe Their Students Will Grow

For the high-impact educator, focusing on student growth has a different look than executing a lesson plan to perfection. The lesson is merely the first pitch, and it leads not to the students' instant and full grasp of the goals but rather to an exposure to content that will require trial, error, feedback, and more trial. The emphasis for high-impact educators is student growth, plain and simple. Everything else, including implementing fresh teaching practices, collaborating effectively with colleagues and administrators, and developing a welcoming environment for students to enjoy the classroom environment are methods to accomplish that.

Student growth. The interviewed participants for this study saved their highest praise for teachers and professors who would not quit on them. Interestingly, these students and recent graduates perceived the relationship they described with their most effective teachers as socially appropriate, academically driven, and individualized. The high-impact educators being described were not teaching in individual environments, however. They work with all their students (sometimes over 150) this impactfully and harmoniously.

This may explain why so many graduates whole-heartedly believe that they were in an exclusive club of their most impactful teacher's favorite students. There is something powerful, even life-changing, about what high-impact educators do with and for their students. Those interviewed assured that it is not about being nice or friendly or funny (although those attributes help the most impactful teachers), but instead these teachers are the most impactful because they absolutely know their content, know how to teach the content, and, most importantly to many of those interviewed, they fully believed the students could do difficult things until the student could actually do those things.

Being experts in their content and knowing how to teach it, the researchers know, is a process that requires continuous learning and reflection. Even high-impact educators do not start out with all the tools, nor do they ever arrive at a point where student growth becomes automatic.

WHAT IT MEANS FOR US

Our Calling Is Student Growth

Our students, of course, want to be known, cared for, respected, even adored. In fact, most K–12 students and many younger college students would choose these feelings over student growth if only one were possible.

Positive relationships are comforting, and most of us want that comfort. Moreover, positive relationships absolutely matter in the educational process. There is an immediate impact to emphasizing harmonious relationships and the potential to greatly affect a student forever. How we interact matters—so much so that K–12 school districts across the country have reimagined schedules, priorities, hiring practices, teacher evaluation, and more to reflect this emphasis on relationships.

It is, after all, the right way to teach. Students will almost certainly learn more, retain more when being taught in a harmonious environment. However, if the learning of difficult concepts and skills do not accompany the great relationships in school, the harmony is truly nothing more significant than short-term pleasure with, perhaps, short-term benefits. High-impact educators use relationship skills as part of their arsenal to teach curriculum, improve student capabilities, and make students work to become more than they once were.

Interestingly, college seniors do not reference friendly, cool, pleasant teachers unless they feel they were pushed to improve by these affable folks. With this, many seniors in college now speak highly of K–12 teachers and coaches they did not necessarily like or enjoy while in their classes. Many college seniors fondly recall teachers who pushed them, made them stretch out of comfort zones, at times even made them angry or frustrated. They recognize and cherish the educators who were invested in their success, despite being too young or immature to recognize or appreciate the lessons being learned while it was happening.

Yes, the most impactful teachers need great relationship skills. As the multitude of student participants in this study have outlined, however, sometimes the relationship needed in the moment is not the relationship a student necessarily desires. The high-impact educator excels with this realization. We are not teaching to make students happy right now and forever in our presence; we are here to make certain students succeed long after they leave us.

The goal is student growth. Whatever it takes. When students leave our classrooms or labs as better readers, writers, mathematicians, nurse practitioners, attorneys, business administrators, and more caring people, they are more apt to fully realize their capacity. Whether students transition to a different grade, a collegiate setting, graduate school, or a profession, they reap the rewards of high-impact educators focusing on their growth and development above all else.

Furthermore, student growth is for all students. Some participants interviewed for this study referenced teachers in their past who played a role in making a college education a reality. Before knowing this teacher, they explained, becoming a college student was no more imagined than becoming an international superstar. The most impactful teachers have a way of making those things possible, the authors have learned.

College is perhaps not for everyone. Growth is. The high-impact educator does not teach to reach a maximum percentage of his or her former students studying in the Ivy League. Rather, the most impactful educators have developed the skills required to awaken students to their possibilities. All students deserve to grow; they deserve to experience the discomforts of the growth zone and the incredible, sometimes life-changing satisfaction and realization of accomplishing something that was impossible the day before.

Those interviewed for this book are proud of one school-related attribute more than anything else: they are most fulfilled by the academic struggles they have overcome. This growth gave them the strength to fight through more discomfort and achieve again, and the cycle became habitual for them. The most significant factor separating high-impact educators is found in those very habits. High-impact educators are dedicated to continuous growth for themselves and their students.

CLOSING PERSPECTIVE

For good reasons, relationships are dominating the discussion in K–12 education today. All of the valid research, all of the student feedback, and everything that makes sense to educational leaders tell us that nothing we know and nothing we attempt to teach will amount to anything with our students until we know them, empathize with them, and communicate with them accordingly. Nothing about this is wrong.

We are doing our students a great disservice, however, if we focus on our relationships with full force while either allowing student growth to be cast aside, or, perhaps just as damaging, assuming that our harmonious relationships somehow translate to student growth. Student growth must be the first goal of education, not an assumption. Relationships? Student growth is impossible without relationships. Yet relationships are entirely possible without student growth. This is the trap.

What does this mean for college departments, school districts, professors, and teachers who emphasize the relationships? Awesome. Students need these relationships; they need to have adults who care and validate and guide. They also need these adults to use the relationships to teach difficult content. They need to learn how to work through discomfort.

What does this mean for university instructors and K–12 teachers who emphasize the curriculum? Glorious. Students need to learn that which is not readily available to them at the moment; they need to be challenged by adults and content that, when learned, will make them more capable and further prepared to learn even more. They also need these adults to positively know them and effectively communicate with them so that learning the curriculum is possible.

The influence that high-impact educators have on their students is paramount. There are endless variables and initiatives within our educational systems including curriculum, learning spaces, building design, technology, schedules, pedagogical models, and assessments; however, these are peripherals.

The participants interviewed for this study were invited to reflect on their experiences in schools and universities to discuss any and all variables that were critical to their success. According to the participants, there is no greater impact in schools on academic achievement and development than caring and competent educators. Long after graduation, the most successful students remember and cherish the teachers who knew and supported them as they emphatically insisted on their growth.

A Note to Parents

The research conducted for this book intends to inform educators within the K–12 and collegiate domains. With that in mind, the authors, combining fifty-plus years of K–12 and higher education experience, conducted and coded over 150 interviews of college graduates with a focused objective to improve the quality of teaching and learning in today's classrooms.

Those interviewed for this study were asked extensive questions about school, their teachers and professors, and the myriad of details related to who the most impactful educators are and what these incredible teachers do. Their responses created the vision and outline of this book. Clearly and undoubtedly, there are high-impact educators who oversee student growth so prolifically, so consistently that educators in the K–12 and university settings are wise to consider their approaches, strategies, and attitudes.

The authors of this book would be remiss, however, if they failed to address a theme that consistently wove itself throughout the fabric of the participants' success in academia and beyond. The most successful students are so often the upshot of purposeful parents, whose emphasis on education, along with other priorities, reverberates to create a lasting path of academic accomplishment. Great students recognize and appreciate high-impact educators, certainly, yet the majority of those interviewed could not detail their most impactful teachers without first crediting the most impactful educators on Earth—parents.

Anyone with substantial experience as an educator (and almost any other reasonable adult) knows that parents play the primary role in the development of their children. The authors of this book, moreover, are not attempting to break news on this front. Research is not required to tell us that parents matter. Kids with great parents are often more receptive to growth opportunities in school, they are more likely to overcome school-related obstacles, and they are endlessly more likely to use school to better their lives. This is not a staggering announcement.

However, the authors did unwrap a few interesting themes perhaps not so obvious as to assume that they are fully recognized by everyone. From the mouths of college freshman, college seniors, and recent college graduates (successful by definition of pursuing academia advancement post high school graduation) come the following observations about the power parents possess in matters related to academics.

PARENTS' INFLUENCE IS OMNIPRESENT AND POTENTIALLY CEASELESS

This was quite telling. "Not going to college was not an option for me." The authors heard scores of interviewees say this or something close to it. Why? "My mom and dad didn't make anything else an option." That is not to say that these students arrived at college against their will while being dragged by their parents. They were not reluctant in the least. Their message conveyed that from an early age, they, with the help of their parents, envisioned themselves going to college to study for a career of their choosing and the preparation to that end was expected.

How many incredibly capable children grow up without those voices at home? As educators we have seen young people transcend very difficult circumstances and home lives to become high-achieving students. Several of the participants in this study came from low socioeconomic backgrounds and many were first-generation college students. They, too, spoke in depth about the vital role of parents and credited their parents as critical sources of support and encouragement throughout their K–12 and college education.

Several interviewed participants insisted they are not smarter than anyone else, including their high school classmates who did not attend a college or university; they simply grew up hearing they will go to college because that will help them find a better life.

Is it necessarily a better life? No, of course not. We know college is not for everyone; we know there are successful adults without college degrees. It can and should be argued, however, that having an option to attend a college or university equates to a better life. Many participants, for example, shared that their parents insisted they attend college because they themselves did not.

Literally everyone is capable of not becoming a college graduate. Only 34 percent of U.S. citizens have a college degree. By definition, they have options that 66 percent of the population do not. Those who interviewed for this book cite parents as the single-most significant determination for those who prove capable and choose to attend university. The influence parents have is boundless—and they will either emphasize education or they will not.

PARENTS OF SUCCESSFUL COLLEGE STUDENTS EXPECT, IF NOT DEMAND, LEARNING AND GROWTH FROM THEIR CHILDREN

To begin, these great parents create an environment where learning becomes habitual. The interviewed participants for this study described their parents as being general managers of the educational process. At first, they provide a head start by reading to and with their children. This evolves to overseeing the completion of homework and eventually to simply being assured that schoolwork and studying is being completed (and learned) adequately. Many participants insisted that becoming a college student was not an accident; rather, it was a process begun by parents until it was eventually owned by the child.

These habits were instilled to be lifelong, according to those interviewed. Great parents do not view education as something to "get through"; they have experienced, whether by benefitting from a life of learning themselves or recognizing its value in those around them, a reality that rewards those who are consistently growing.

Although no participant for this study actually said the words "American Dream," countless described the ideology as being a priority within their homes. The most fundamental tenant of the American Dream is that we adults raise our children so that their lives are better than ours. Many interviewees explained that one or both of their parents did not attend college and, as a result, insisted that their children would have the opportunity they did not. "My mom and dad were smart enough to go to college—but they didn't. There was no way I wasn't going to be a college graduate."

Although vastly varied as individuals, parents of successful college students commonly emphasize the following at home:

- faith;
- family;
- community/friendships;
- financial independence and security; and
- education.

These pronounced themes emerged throughout the interview process for this book, and it reveals something truly significant about how the parents of highly educated children think. Education is not a "thing" for these great parents; it is not a nuisance, a chore, or even an obligation. Education, rather, is a core value, something worthy of holding a place at the table with faith, family, and community and friendship.

Everything is improved when education as well as loving relationships are valued. Over and over, the college students and recent college graduates interviewed for this book explained that their successful educational history was anything but lucky. So often, their path toward academic growth was guided before they knew enough to recognize the benefits.

Educators and every adult within our educational systems share a sacred relationship with parents. We are wise to nurture those relationships and partner whenever possible to strengthen our collective support of the students we share. The path to college graduation is ultimately accomplished by the hard work of determined students working with high-impact educators, but their journey is first forged with the strong influence of great parents.

About the Authors

Dr. John Tufte has taught in secondary and higher education for over twenty years and has served as a dean, principal, and K–12 superintendent. He is a 2012 Outstanding Faculty of the Year recipient and writes and speaks to educators, administrators, and parents on educational leadership, coaching, youth sports, and K–12 curriculum and instruction.

Dr. Brenda Tufte has taught in K–12 and higher education for over twenty-five years and is a professor and chair in graduate education, overseeing programs in teacher leadership and educational leadership and administration. She writes and leads professional development in K–12 and higher education and is the 2012 North Dakota Teacher of the Year, 2014 NEA Foundation Global Fellow, and 2017 Crystal Apple Award recipient for Outstanding Post-Secondary Educator.

Made in the USA
Coppell, TX
16 July 2021